Shannon Fry 2011
For 11th birthday from Jack,
Jo and Smoky the cat

Humphrey's World of Pets

Praise for *The World According to Humphrey*:

'A charming, feel-good tale.' *Irish Times*

'A breezy, well-crafted first novel. Humphrey's matter-of-fact, table-level view of the world is alternately silly and profound and Birney captures his unique blend of innocence and earnestness from the start.' *Publisher's Weekly*

Praise for *Friendship According to Humphrey*:

'An effective exploration of the joys and pains of making and keeping friends, which will strike a chord with many children.' *Daily Telegraph*

Praise for *Trouble According to Humphrey*:

'Children fall for Humphrey, and you can't beat him for feelgood life lessons.' *Sunday Times*

Humphrey's World of Pets

Betty G. Birney worked at Disneyland and the Disney Studios, has written numerous children's television shows and is the author of over thirty-five books, including the best-selling *The World According to Humphrey*, which won the Richard and Judy Children's Book Club, *Friendship According to Humphrey*, *Trouble According to Humphrey*, *Surprises According to Humphrey*, *More Adventures According to Humphrey* and *Holidays According to Humphrey*. Her work has won many awards, including an Emmy and three Humanitas Prizes. She lives in America with her husband.

Have you read all of Humphrey's adventures?

The World According to Humphrey
Friendship According to Humphrey
Trouble According to Humphrey
Adventure According to Humphrey
(special publication for World Book Day 2008)
Surprises According to Humphrey
More Adventures According to Humphrey
Holidays According to Humphrey
School According to Humphrey
Humphrey's Big-Big-Big Book of Stories (3 books in 1)
Humphrey's Great-Great-Great Book of Stories (3 books in 1)

Humphrey's Book of Fun-Fun-Fun
Humphrey's Ha-Ha-Ha Joke Book

Humphrey's Tiny Tales
My Pet Show Panic!
My Treasure Hunt Trouble!
(special publication for World Book Day 2011)
My Summer Fair Surprise!
My Creepy-Crawly Camping Adventure!

By the same author
The Princess and the Peabodys

Humphrey's World of Pets

Betty G. Birney

Compiled by Amanda Li

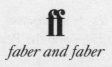

faber and faber

First published in 2011
by Faber and Faber Limited
Bloomsbury House, 74–77 Great Russell Street
London WC1B 3DA

Printed and bound by CPI Group (UK) Ltd, Croydon, CR0 4YY

Graphic design by Ali Walper

A CIP record for this book
is available from the British Library

ISBN 978–0–571–27026–2

2 4 6 8 10 9 7 5 3 1

A NOTE FROM BETTY

One of the happiest days of Humphrey's life was when he left Pet-O-Rama and came to Room 26 of Longfellow School to be a classroom hamster.

Choosing a pet is fun, but it's important to choose the pet that's right for you and to know how to take care of it *before* you bring it home.

We've rounded up the best information possible on selecting and taking care of a variety of pets and added Humphrey's personal thoughts, jokes, and fun activities, too.

I hope this book helps you and your pet become the perfect pair so you'll have many happy times together – just like Humphrey and his friends!

Betty G. Birney

CONTENTS

My Pet Profile 10

Happy Hamsters 18

Rodents Rule 38

Marvellous Mice 40

Gorgeous Gerbils 45

Cute Chinchillas 50

Great Guinea Pigs 59

More Stuff About Rodents 67

Joking Around with Humphrey 74

Humphrey's Rodent Fun 76

Cuddly Rabbits 82

Joking Around with Humphrey 95

Humphrey's Rabbit Fun 97

Clever Cats 102

Joking Around with Humphrey 118

Humphrey's Cat Fun 120

Dashing Dogs 124

Joking Around with Humphrey 140

Humphrey's Dog Fun 142

Fascinating Fish 146

Joking Around with Humphrey 159

Humphrey's Fishy Fun 161

Unusual Pets 167

Joking Around with Humphrey 184

Humphrey's Unusual Pet Fun 186

Humphrey's Amazing Pets 193

My Star Pet 205

Answers 210

MY PET PROFILE

My pet is a _Kitten / Cat_

~~His~~/her name is _Minstral_

_____

I called my pet this name because
She is the same coular
_____
_____

My pet is _1 on May 16th 2012_ years old

Things we do to celebrate my pet's
birthday _Pamper her_
_____
_____

My pet personality

Which words would you use to describe your pet?
Circle the ones that apply.

MISCHIEVOUS   QUIET   ADORABLE

WISE

CUTE   PLAYFUL   SMELLY   FRIENDLY

WILD   INTELLIGENT

TIMID

CRAZY

SWEET   LOVING

HAPPY   LOYAL

Can you think of any others?
What are the things that you love about your pet?

cudely
_____
_____
_____
_____

My pet portrait

What does your pet look like? Is he/she soft and fluffy, colourful or scaly, small or large? What colour are your pet's eyes? Write your description here.

Mintral has soft and cluffy fur. She has rings round her tail stripes all over her body white on her neck and jin and the rest of her body is brown with grey throw it and spots on her tummy and eyes amber

I have soft fur, dark, inquisitive eyes and a little pink nose. Humans usually say I'm CUTE!

Draw a picture of your pet
or glue a photograph in the box.

My pet's favourite things

> Oh life is just so full of FAVOURITE things! Where do I start? My wonderful whizzy wheel, the lovely Golden Miranda, tasty Nutri-Nibbles, my little notebook and pen... I'm running out of space here!

What are your pet's favourite things?

cuddles, toys and fluffy things (and also her mummy witch is me)

Things my pet doesn't like!

loud nouses like a bang

Pets make you feel good!

Owning a pet is a very special thing. Animals keep us company, make us laugh and give us lots of love and affection. Animal experts know that having a pet is a good thing. Most of us feel happier and more relaxed when we are spending time with a pet and we may even be healthier as a result. Taking care of a pet is very satisfying and teaches us a lot about responsibility – as well as being a whole lot of fun!

You can learn a LOT about yourself by taking care of another species!

Looking after an animal has other benefits too. Animals are great listeners and, like Aldo, Mrs Brisbane and all the children in Room 26, you might find that telling your pet your worries can really help you work things out.

> **Humans are always talking to me about their problems. And even though I can only SQUEAK-SQUEAK-SQUEAK in return, talking to me certainly seems to make them feel better.**

Whatever pet you own or choose, he or she will soon become part of the family and you won't be able to imagine life without your little friend!

Thinking about a pet?

You may already have a pet of your own, or perhaps you are just thinking about getting one. If that's the case, finding the right pet to suit you and your family will be a big decision. You'll need to find out as much as you can about the animal: what it eats, where it lives, how it behaves and a whole lot more. Read on to find out more about looking after different pets and which kind might be right for you.

Not everyone takes to pets at first. Mrs Brisbane didn't seem to like me at all when we first met. She wanted to take me back to the pet shop! Now she's one of my FAVOURITE humans — and I'm pretty sure she loves me too.

HAPPY HAMSTERS

Hamsters are one of the most popular and appealing pets around. They're friendly, active and very, very cute!

YES-YES-YES, I agree!

There are several different varieties of hamster but the most usual type that is kept as a pet is the Syrian or Golden Hamster. It is sometimes known as the Teddy Bear Hamster because of its golden-brown fur.

That's ME!

But despite the 'golden' name, Syrian Hamsters come in many other colours – cream, white, darker brown, patterned – and also different coat types, such as smooth, satin and longhaired.

Other hamsters commonly kept as pets are the smaller Chinese Hamsters and Russian Hamsters. Russian Hamsters are also known as Dwarf Hamsters because of their size. Make sure you know whether your pet is a Golden Hamster or a Dwarf Hamster – it's an important difference!

Hamsters prefer to sleep during the daytime which, of course, is when humans are up and about. This has led some people to think that hamsters sleep all the time or that they might even be a little lazy, but this just isn't the case.

> Certainly not!
> I am always BUSY-BUSY-BUSY! There's food to store, wheels to spin, burrowing to do, and of course my human friends keep me unsqueakably busy with all their different needs.

But when they are awake, which is mainly at night-time, dawn and dusk, hamsters are incredibly active and busy creatures.

You only have to watch one in action, furiously spinning around on its wheel, climbing up the sides of its cage, digging and running around to see this!

> **Important:** Never disturb a sleeping hamster. You might be tempted to wake your hamster for a play when it is napping during the day but this really isn't fair. Would you like it if somebody suddenly woke you up in the middle of a sleep? Don't be surprised if your hamster gets grumpy and tries to nip you if he is suddenly disturbed!

A home for your hamster

There are many different types of hamster cages. Some are made of clear plastic, others have bars and some even have extra features, such as tunnels leading from one cage area to another. Whichever kind you choose, make sure it is nice and spacious, with something for your hamster to climb on and to run along, like ramps. Wire cages are often recommended for the larger Syrian hamsters

because they can use the bars to climb and exercise.
If you have a new hamster, gently introduce
him to his new home. Make sure he has food
and water, then leave him alone for at least 24 hours.
Hamsters really need this time by themselves to settle
down. There'll be plenty of time for hamster fun when
your pet has got used to its new surroundings.

I remember when I first
arrived at Lower-Your-Voice-
A.J.'s house. Everyone was shouting
and I just wanted to squeak
PLEASE-PLEASE-PLEASE
be quiet!

Shhhhh

Cosy cages

Your cage will need sawdust spread on the bottom, topped with layers of kitchen paper, hay and cardboard. Your hamster will love having plenty of material that he can shred with his teeth and burrow into. The cage will also need different areas where your hamster can have time alone, sleep, burrow, go to the toilet and store his food. Hamsters like to hide away at times and they prefer to sleep inside enclosed spaces, so you'll need a small box with an entrance hole for a cosy bed. Pad the box with kitchen roll, cloth, hay or special bedding from the pet shop.

Golden Hamsters really prefer to be on their own and shouldn't be kept with other hamsters. They are different from Dwarf Hamsters, who like to live in pairs – but make sure they are of the same sex or they will have babies.

As you know, I'm an EXTREMELY friendly hamster — but when it comes to my cage, I like my own space!

House warming

Hamsters like it best in quite warm temperatures – no lower than 18 °C/65 °F. But make sure the cage is not in direct sunlight as your pet will get uncomfortably hot. However, if the temperature gets too cold, your hamster may feel the need to hibernate. So, if the temperature has dropped and you find your hamster curled up in a ball, feeling chilly to the touch and breathing very weakly, this could be the reason. Try gently warming your pet in your hands to slowly wake him. He may shake and shiver once he starts to wake up, but the best thing to do is to place him back in his cage, somewhere warm and quiet.

Cheeky hamsters

One of the most noticeable things about a hamster is his habit of storing food. He has special pouches inside his cheeks designed for this very purpose. A hamster with his cheeks full of food will look like he has a very full and puffy face. But why do hamsters do this? In the wild, hamsters may have to survive for long periods without much food, so they store it to carry back to their underground homes. Also, hamsters can be vulnerable to predators so it is safer for them to carry the food back to their underground burrow than to try to eat it outside. So don't be surprised if your pet spends hours moving bits of food and bedding into 'safe' places. He's a natural hoarder!

Hamsters' cheeks can actually hold an incredible amount. In fact, hamsters are able to carry up to half their body weight in food just by using their pouches!

If I look a little PUFFY today it's because I'm saving my lunch to take back to my sleeping house!

However, a puffy face may also be a sign that your hamster feels scared or threatened, as when hamsters feel intimidated they will often puff up their cheeks.

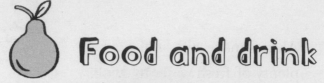

Food and drink

Hamsters need hard food such as seeds, grains and nuts to nibble and gnaw on. You can buy special hamster mixes in pet shops and leave these in a small bowl for the hamster to help himself. Hamsters also enjoy fresh fruit and vegetables. Chopped up pieces of cabbage, broccoli, apple and pear will usually go down well. Pieces of carrot and even dog biscuits will be a nice treat for gnawing on. Most food will be stored inside your hamster's pouches and hidden in his special hoarding place for another time.

Aldo sometimes gives me tiny dog biscuits. That makes me HAPPY-HAPPY-HAPPY!

Always make sure your pet has
plenty of fresh water to drink.
Most hamsters have a drinking bottle
of water, positioned just outside the
bars of the cage, which can be sucked
via a small tube.

Playtime!

Hamsters need lots of activity. They love to explore
and are very curious little creatures.

There are all sorts of pet 'toys' that can be bought
from shops but you don't need to spend lots of money
to have fun with your hamster. It only takes a few
items to create an exciting environment for your
playful pet.

Play ideas

✳ Give your hamster a toilet-roll tube 'tunnel' and he will have lots of fun running backwards and forwards through it.

✳ He will also like a cardboard egg box, which he can use as a climbing toy.

✳ Twigs are good for climbing on and also for gnawing.

✳ Try hiding food and the occasional treat in different parts of the cage. Your hamster will have to search around for his food, which should keep him busy and happy for quite a while.

✳ A hamster ball for use outside the cage is also a good buy as it will give your hamster plenty of exercise and is great fun for you to watch and follow around the room.

I'm having a ball!

✱ A wheel is a must, of course. Make sure the wheel you get is the type that is solid, because the ones with little gaps in them can trap your pet's limbs. Your hamster will spend hours running around his little wheel and it will give him lots of exercise.

> Great ideas! I also
> LOVE-LOVE-LOVE my little
> mirror. It comes in handy to check
> my grooming and I can hide my
> notebook behind it. Perhaps your
> hamster would like
> one, too?

Take it gently

Hamsters are lovely to hold but, like any animals, they need time to get used to you and to being held and touched. If your new hamster tries to nip you, he is probably nervous, so patience will be needed. Place your hand gently inside the cage to begin with, so that he gets used to your smell (and the sight of a giant hand coming into his house!). Then, stroke the hamster when he is awake inside his cage and also hand feed him from time to time. Gradually, he should get used to your contact and will be fine about being held.

Escape!

It's good to let your pet run around outside the cage now and again. But remember that small rodents are skilful escape artists so they must be watched carefully. It's all too easy to lose sight of your pet and he may disappear somewhere in the house. So when you let your pet out of his cage, choose a space for him to run around in that doesn't have holes in the floor or cracks in the skirting board where he could squeeze through. Pets can disappear up chimneys and behind furniture too.

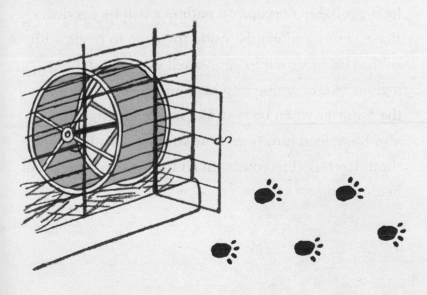

Anti-escape tips

* Try to create a safe play area by using books as 'walls' to contain your hamster.
* Always watch your pet as he scurries around and gently place him back in the safe area if he tries to run off.
* Once he's back in the cage, make sure that the door is secure and won't come open easily. Also remember not to leave the door open!

> I've managed to get out of my cage many times because of its special LOCK-THAT-DOESN'T-LOCK. I wonder if any other hamsters can do this!

Clever Mr Morales once lured me back into my cage with a trail of sunflower seeds. They were so TASTY-TASTY-TASTY!

If the worst happens and your pet gets lost in the house, try this tip to lure him back. Leave the cage open on the floor with a tasty snack inside, or try leaving a trail of favourite food leading to the cage. Leave the cage alone for a few hours and hopefully your pet will be tempted to get back in.

Hamster facts

✱ Golden or Syrian Hamsters originally come from the hot, dry deserts of Syria in the Middle East.

✱ Hamsters have poor eyesight but a very good sense of smell.

✱ Hamsters have a scent gland on each hip, which you might be able to see if you look carefully. These scent glands are used to mark their territory and attract mates.

✱ Experts believe that all pet Golden Hamsters are descended from one female hamster, which was captured from the wild in Syria, in 1930.

✱ Hamsters are natural burrowers. In the wild, their burrows are often very long with several entrances and special places for nesting, for storing food and for 'toilets'. A hamster burrow can be as deep as two metres!

✱ Hamsters are usually described as nocturnal creatures – active during the night and sleepy during the day. But, in fact, hamsters are what's called crepuscular. This means they are particularly active at

dawn and dusk. As humans are diurnal
(we like to sleep at night) you may find that your
energetic hamster makes quite a lot of noise while
you're trying to sleep!

Here's a useful tip. If you want
a good night's sleep,
get a wheel that
doesn't SQUEAK!

RODENTS RULE

Hamsters are a member of a group called rodents.
Rodents are mammals that have something special
about their teeth. Their incisors – the teeth at the very
front of the mouth – keep on growing throughout
their lives. That's why these kinds of pets spend a lot
of time chewing on things, to keep their teeth short. If
they don't, their teeth can get so long that they can't
feed properly.

Other common pets that belong to the rodent family are mice, gerbils and guinea pigs. Pet rats are popular, too. Much of the advice about hamsters applies to all small rodents, but there are some areas in which they differ. So let's take a closer look at some of these other furry friends.

At Pet-O-Rama, rodents were all put together in the Small Pet Department. There was a LOT-LOT-LOT of excited squeaking going on whenever customers came in. I'm proud to say that Ms Mac chose me because she thought I was 'the most intelligent and handsome hamster' in the shop!

MARVELLOUS MICE

There are many different types of pet mice. There are fancy mice, which come in a variety of colours, spiny mice, which have bristly fur, and even zebra mice, which, you've guessed it, are stripy! Whichever kind you choose, you'll find mice need plenty of opportunities to run around and to build themselves nests. As mice are quite small, the best kind of home for them is a glass or plastic tank with a mesh lid. An old fish tank makes a pretty effective mouse house. Cover the bottom of the tank with newspaper, then place plenty of hay and kitchen paper on top. This will allow your mouse to make a little nest − she will like to shred up the kitchen roll to make her own nesting material.

Mice also need time alone to get used to their new home. They are very sociable animals and like to have company so you can have two mice living together − but, as with all pets, make sure they are not a male and a female or they may have babies.

Be especially careful of mice escaping – they are renowned for squeezing themselves into tiny gaps and spaces!

Handling a mouse

If you handle your mouse regularly, she should eventually become tame. Remember to be calm and gentle and take care not to damage your mouse's delicate tail. Pick your mouse up by gently lifting her around the middle and cupping her in your hands. Never pick up a mouse by her tail.

Some people are better at handling than others. I love it when SPEAK-UP-SAYEH holds me in her hand. She's so gentle that it makes me feel as if I am floating on a cloud!

Feeding

Mice can be fed on special rodent pellets or mixes from your pet shop. You can occasionally give your mouse small amounts of fresh fruits and vegetables (greens, apple, carrot) as a treat. She will enjoy seeds such as sunflower seeds but do not give these too often as they contain quite a lot of fat. A gnawing food block from a pet shop will give your mouse plenty to chew on.

Oh yes, we rodents like to gnaw. In fact we gnaw such a lot that we should probably all go and visit the country of 'GNAW-WAY'!

Mouse facts

✷ Mice can be found in all corners of the globe, even in chilly Antarctica.

✷ The tail of a mouse is usually as long as her body.

✷ Mice squeak at very high frequencies, so high that humans often cannot hear them.

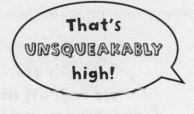

That's UNSQUEAKABLY high!

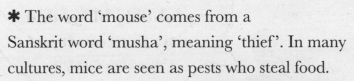

✷ The word 'mouse' comes from a Sanskrit word 'musha', meaning 'thief'. In many cultures, mice are seen as pests who steal food.

✷ In Roman times, the naturalist Pliny wrote down many of his remedies for illnesses. One of them advised parents to feed their children boiled mice, to help stop them wetting the bed!

✳ People have long thought that mice like cheese. But this just isn't true. Mice actually have a sweet tooth and are more attracted to foods high in sugar. As this fact is becoming more widely known, people have started to use chocolate instead of cheese on mouse traps!

But please DON'T feed your rodents chocolate or cheese! We much prefer healthy treats like fruit and veggies.

GORGEOUS GERBILS

Gerbils are curious, friendly animals that just love to dig. A gerbil has quite large hind legs in relation to his body and he moves with a hopping motion. He also has a long hairy tail that helps him balance when he is standing on his hind legs.

In the wild, gerbils dig tunnels underground. So your pet gerbil will need plenty of wood shavings and bedding for burrowing and digging. Like other rodents, gerbils will also appreciate an exercise wheel (solid), something to play with and a gnawing block.

Plastic cages can't be used for gerbils as they will gnaw through them very quickly. A specially designed gerbil cage is the best option. A glass tank can also be used, with a wire mesh lid fitted on top to allow ventilation. If you choose this option, make sure the tank is very well covered and fastened at all times. Gerbils are great climbers and jumpers and will easily escape!

I love to climb and jump too. I like to swing myself across my bridge ladder and sometimes I hang from my tree branch with one paw. I am a daring young hamster on a flying trapeze. WHEE!

In the wild, gerbils live in groups and they are much happier in company. So it's a good idea to have more than one gerbil as they appreciate friends. Again, make sure they are in same-sex pairs.

As gerbils love to hop and jump you could also provide an 'exercise yard' for your gerbil that allows him plenty of room to run around. Gerbils are usually frightened of large, open spaces but they will love playing in a run that contains things like boxes, flowerpots, cardboard tubes and logs.

Important: You must never hold or pull a gerbil's tail as it could break off.

Gerbil facts

✱ In the wild, gerbils don't take water baths – they have sand baths instead! You can give your gerbil his very own sand bath. Put some clean sand into a box and let your gerbil roll around in it. He should love it and it will help keep his coat healthy.

✱ Gerbils use their sharp claws to burrow, creating networks of tunnels which allow the gerbil to stay underground for long periods of time. The tunnels also protect them from the extreme temperatures of the desert and help them quickly disappear if there is a dangerous predator above ground.

* Most pet gerbils are Mongolian gerbils. In the wild, they live in the deserts of Mongolia. Gerbils are also found in the sandy plains of Africa, Asia and the Middle East.

* When a gerbil is frightened or excited, he thumps its back legs, which helps warns his friends of any danger.

> I'm not a thumper.
> If I feel unsafe I'll rise up
> on my back legs and sniff the air
> to see what's around. If I'm scared,
> I might puff out my cheeks.
> And if I'm REALLY terrified
> I may even play
> dead!

* The Latin name for gerbils, *Meriones unguiculatus*, means 'clawed warrior'.

CUTE CHINCHILLAS

Chinchillas are another member of the rodent family and they are well-known for their beautiful, soft fur which comes in shades of grey, beige, white and black. They are quite large creatures, about the size of a rabbit, with big ears and bushy tails. Some people think that chinchillas look like a cross between a giant cuddly mouse and a squirrel! In the wild, the chinchilla's large ears help her to hear very well and to be warned of any danger. Her long hind legs enable her to move very quickly if frightened.

Behaviour and play

Chinchillas are inquisitive creatures and investigate things by chewing. One of the first things a chinchilla will do in a new environment, or when given a new toy, is to chew on it.

I have a **GREAT** idea.
Why not rotate your pet's toys,
offering her one or two toys the first
week, then swapping them for different
ones the next? It's always nice
to have a surprise toy that
you haven't played with
in a long time!

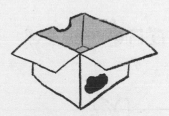

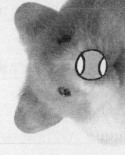

A chinchilla will like all the usual rodent toys but don't give her plastic toys as these may splinter when chewed on. A cardboard box with holes cut in it is fun for a chinchilla to explore.

Most chinchillas don't like being cuddled a lot, but they will let you hold them once they get to know you. They will often jump and crawl on you if you sit nearby, but sudden moves and loud noises will scare them off.

I'm not crazy about loud noises either. When Og first went 'BOING!' I nearly jumped out of my furry skin!

Boing!

Keeping a chinchilla

Chinchillas are natural rock hoppers that like to scurry around so they need lots of exercise. Because of this they need to be kept in an enclosure or a room with lots of floor space and they will need time outside their enclosure every day to have a good run around. A chinchilla enclosure should be at least 2m wide x 1m deep x 2m high (about 6.5ft x 3.5ft x 6.5ft) and must be even bigger if you have more than one chinchilla. It needs to be made of strong non-toxic wire (not wood, your pet will chew through it) and it should have different levels inside so that your pet can jump and climb. The cage floor also needs to be made of a material that the chinchilla can't chew through. If wire mesh flooring is used, the chinchilla should have some solid platforms and branches to spend time on, otherwise she may injure her feet. You can put wood shavings on the floor of the enclosure as well as hay, straw or shredded paper. Provide a nest box where your chinchilla can hide away when she wants to.

As chinchillas are sociable animals you can keep more than one together, but the usual rule about the same sex applies!

Chewy chinchillas

Chinchillas are incredibly chewy creatures and will gnaw on just about everything – so be very careful and don't let your pet near electrical wires when she is running around. Also bear in mind that she will probably bite and chew things around the house like skirting boards, plants and wallpaper!

Put some things in her enclosure that can be safely chewed, such as untreated apple or pear branches. A gnawing block is a good idea, as this will help your chinchilla wear her teeth down.

Keeping cool and clean

As chinchillas have very thick furry coats and cannot sweat, they can get over-hot very quickly. Their environment and enclosure must be kept nice and cool.

What do you call a cold chinchilla? CHIN-CHILLY!

Chinchillas, like gerbils, keep themselves clean in the wild by having sand baths. Your pet chinchilla will need a bath every other day in special dust to keep her fur clean and grease-free. You can buy special chinchilla sand and a suitable bath from a pet shop. The dust bath should be large enough for the chinchilla to roll around in. Put about five cm (two inches) of sand inside the bath – then let things roll! About ten minutes is usually long enough.

Feeding

Chinchillas need lots of good-quality hay or grass to eat. They can also eat special chinchilla nuggets bought from a pet shop – follow the instructions on how much to feed. Don't give chinchillas any of the special pet mixes from the shop as they are very choosy and will only pick out the best bits! Very small amounts of fresh vegetables and fruits can also be given, including apple, carrot, potato, pumpkin, celery and sweet potato. Be careful not to over-feed your pet or give too many snacks high in fat or sugar such as raisins and sunflower seeds.

Chinchilla facts

* Chinchillas originally come from South America, where they live in rock crevices and burrows. They were named after the Chincha Indians, who made clothes from their warm fur.

✱ Chinchillas were once at risk of becoming extinct because their skins were often used to make expensive fur coats. It can take more than one hundred chinchilla skins to make a single fur coat! Today it is illegal to hunt wild chinchillas.

✱ Like hamsters, chinchillas are crepuscular, which means they are at their most active in the evening and early morning. Bear in mind that if your pet's enclosure is close to your bedroom, you may be woken up very early in the morning by lots of noise, as chinchillas are very active!

Chinchillas are my kind of rodent! I like an early start to the day as well. But I try my best not to make TOO much noise so that my human friends can sleep.

Shhhh

✳ If a chinchilla is caught by a predator in the wild, one of the ways in which she defends herself is to suddenly shed fur. This helps her to escape and find somewhere to hide until the predator has gone. This 'fur slip' can also happen if you handle your chinchilla in a way she doesn't like.

✳ Chinchilla fur is thought to be the softest in the world. It is so dense that fleas and other parasites cannot live on it.

Wow! I'd like to stroke a chinchilla — it must feel 'FURRY' soft!

✳ Chinchillas are excellent jumpers and can jump up to 1.8m (6ft)!

GREAT GUINEA PIGS

Guinea pigs are plump, furry and adorable. Bigger than hamsters, they can sometimes grow up to over 30cm (12–13 inches) long, though many are smaller than this. In their natural surroundings, guinea pigs have long brown or grey fur. Pet guinea pigs, however, can come in a combination of colours: brown, black, reddish or white. Some are longhaired and others have short hair.

A happy home

Most guinea pigs are kept in hutches. It is important that the hutch is large enough for the guinea pig – it should be at least four to five times the length of the guinea pig, with space for sleeping, eating and running around. Living in a hutch means that your guinea pig can live outside in a garden for a good part of the year, though be very careful that the hutch is sturdy and well protected from any predators. And, of course, don't leave the door open!

Guinea pigs need lots of exercise so you must provide a run for your pet. Guinea pigs are often nervous of large, open spaces but will enjoy scurrying around an enclosed run that contains playthings such as boxes, flowerpots and logs. Large plastic pipes make great hiding places and excellent tunnels. You can also let your pet run on the grass in the summer, but keep a careful eye on him. You don't want your pet to disappear!

We rodents just LOVE to explore. One of the most fun times I ever had was on Miranda's desk, roaming among the paper clips, pencils and rubber bands.

DIARY

Keep Out

When it starts to get cold in the autumn/winter, move the hutch inside or into a sheltered place like a garage. You will also need to organise an indoor run area for your pet to make sure he gets his daily exercise.

Inside the hutch plenty of clean fresh bedding will be needed. Good-quality grass hay is ideal. Eating the long hay strands keeps guinea pigs' digestive systems moving and helps prevent their teeth from over-growing.

Feeding your guinea pig

It's very important to know that, just like humans, guinea pigs do not make their own vitamin C. They get this mainly from fresh vegetables so it is very important to make sure that they have enough. Offer your guinea pig a good variety of veggies such as lettuce, cabbage, parsley, spinach, a small piece of carrot, tomato, green or red pepper. Provide these twice a day, morning and evening. Guinea pigs will also enjoy most fruits; try small amounts of banana, blueberry, melon or strawberry.

Pets are like people — they like some foods better than others. Personally I just love chunks of apple and Nutri-Nibbles. You'll soon find out what YOUR pet likes best.

They will also need special guinea pig pellets (some have extra vitamin C added). You can leave a ceramic bowl of these pellets inside their hutch for them to feed on when they wish.

Do not give guinea pigs nuts, seeds or dried fruit. Potatoes, raw beans, flowers and leaves should also be avoided as they can be poisonous to guinea pigs.

Important: The rolling balls that they make for hamsters to run around in **CANNOT** be used for guinea pigs. Some pet shops sell balls for guinea pigs but these aren't a good idea as they can injure your pet's back and feet.

A pair of pigs

In the wild, guinea pigs are sociable and live in groups. Your guinea pig would probably enjoy the company of another, but they must have enough space – you will need a much larger hutch for two guinea pigs. Also it is probably best to get two girl guinea pigs, as two boys may sometimes fight. Males and females together will have lots of babies, unless the male pig is neutered.

(See What is neutering? page 92).

Grooming

This is especially important if your guinea pig is longhaired – you'll need to groom him every day to keep his fur soft and healthy. You can use a soft toothbrush for this. Once he is used to you, a guinea pig will sit happily on your lap while you give him a brush. A treat like a piece of carrot to munch on will also go down well!

Treats – did you say 'Treats'? I LOVE-LOVE-LOVE them!

Guinea pig facts

❋ Guinea pigs come from South America, where they live in burrows and caves in mountains and grassland areas. They were introduced to Europe in the 16th century by the Spanish after they conquered the Incas. Wild guinea pigs still live in countries such as Peru, Ecuador and Argentina.

❋ Guinea pigs are diurnal, like humans. So they are awake during the day and asleep at night.

❋ Guinea pigs make a distinct 'wheeking' or whistling sound when excited.

I hear that the class in Room 14 of Longfellow School have guinea pigs. I'd really like to meet them some day – we could 'WHEEK' and 'SQUEAK' together!

✱ The oldest known pet guinea pig lived to the age of 14 and was called Snowball. She lived in Nottinghamshire, England.

Now, I'm guessing that Snowball was a WHITE guinea pig. They don't call me the smartest hamster in Humphreyville for nothing!

✱ No one is quite sure where the name 'guinea pig' came from. It's possible that the animals were given this name because they were once sold for a guinea (a gold coin). Perhaps 'pig' came from the fact that they sometimes squeal and grunt like pigs!

MORE STUFF ABOUT RODENTS

Here are some general points that apply to all hamsters, mice, gerbils and guinea pigs.

✱ Be very careful not to drop your pet, as small rodents can easily get injured. Never run around while holding a pet – it's best to sit down.

> I learnt from Mrs Brisbane that gravity is a force that pulls us towards the ground. I find that a little scary! So keep your pets safe and DON'T let us fall.

✻ Get your pet slowly used to being handled and always touch him gently, making sure you are supporting all of the creature's weight. Never squeeze your pet. Take things slowly and gain his trust.

✻ Make sure that hamsters, mice and other rodents are kept away from cats and dogs. They may scare, harm or even kill your pet.

As you know, I've had a few close shaves myself. Humans may love cats and dogs — but rodents usually DON'T!

* Keep all cages, hutches and tanks out of direct sunlight and away from draughts.
* Make sure your rodent has the right food and plenty of clean water every day.
* All rodents' teeth grow continuously and they need to gnaw on something to keep them down. Give your pet a block of wood to use as a gnawing block or buy a special block from a pet shop.
* Don't use wood shavings made from cedar or pine in the cage or tank as these can be harmful to rodents.

Clean-up time

Would you want to live in a wet, dirty mess with poo all over the place? Your answer will most likely be a 'No', and your pet would certainly agree with you. Keeping your pet's home clean and dry can be a chore but it must be done regularly.

We like to keep our poo away from our food — who doesn't? So we need a convenient space for a 'potty corner' in our cage. Remember to clean it out EVERY day!

Every day: Use a scoop to take out any droppings and old bits of food. Feed your pet and top up levels of food, if necessary. Wash and refill the water bottle.

Once a week: Thoroughly clean the tank or cage. Take out all the bedding (straw, paper, etc.) then use a cloth with warm water and mild detergent to wash out. You can buy pet-safe cleaning liquids from pet shops. Wait until dry, then replace the bedding and other materials with clean stuff. Wash out the food bowls and water bottles and refill. Remember to always wash your hands well afterwards.

You will probably need to take out your pet and put him somewhere safe while you are doing the cleaning, perhaps in a box.

Golden Miranda is the best cage cleaner ever — and she never says 'Yuck!' about my little potty corner. I REALLY appreciate that.

Have a riot with your rodent!

Rodents are really fun pets to own. So why not make life even more interesting and build your pet an obstacle course? Use things you can find around the house like books, boxes, clean yogurt pots, toys, cardboard tubes, etc. to construct a mini obstacle course.

You can build fences to climb, tunnels to run through and ramps to go up and down. Maybe add a few food treats to pick up for rewards along the way. Your pet will love this new challenge!

Oh, I remember that Mr and Mrs Brisbane did this for me once. It was the best thing EVER! They seemed to have a lot of fun making the obstacle course, too!

Rodent health

If you are worried about your pet for any reason, you should take him to your vet in a secure box or container. Signs that something isn't right with your rodent may include dull-looking eyes, matted fur, weight loss, shaking, runny nose and diarrhoea.

Some of the most common problems
that vets see in small rodents are injuries that are caused
by falling. So be careful – do not allow your pets to run
around freely on high tables and always hold them very
carefully. If you think your pet may be injured, return to
him to his cage first of all to let him recover quietly for a
while. He may be in shock but if he still appears unwell
after an hour or so, take him to the vet.

Dr Drew, my vet, is
a lovely, gentle lady. When I
went for a check-up she looked
at my eyes with a tiny torch, weighed
me on a scale and also listened to my
heart. She EVEN checked my poo!
She said I was one healthy,
handsome hamster.

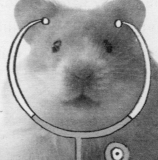

JOKING AROUND WITH HUMPHREY

Q. What do you get if you cross a mouse with a Roman Emperor?
A. Julius Cheeser.

Q. Has a hamster ever been President of the US?
A. Of course - Abrahamster Lincoln.

Q. What did the guinea pig say to the carrot?
A. 'Been nice gnawing you!'

These jokes are just UN-FUR-GETTABLE!

Q. How do hamsters run?

A. Wheely fast.

Q. What's brown, furry and goes up and down?

A. A gerbil in a lift.

Q. Which side of a chinchilla has the most fur?

A. The outside.

Q. What do you give a sick mouse?

A. Mouse-to-mouse resuscitation.

Q. What's grey and has a trunk?

A. A mouse going on holiday.

HUMPHREY'S RODENT FUN

Furry fun wordsearch

As you know, we rodents just LOVE to hide away! Can you find six pets hiding in this wordsearch? The words might be up, down, diagonal — or even backwards!

O	E	I	M	J	G	F	R	G	C
L	M	O	U	S	E	B	I	A	H
A	N	P	T	S	E	P	R	H	I
S	T	I	B	B	A	R	E	J	N
B	C	H	F	E	R	K	T	L	C
O	B	D	N	W	M	I	S	C	H
M	E	I	L	L	V	T	M	N	I
B	U	S	A	Q	U	A	A	H	L
G	E	R	B	I	L	G	H	D	L
I	C	P	G	X	E	A	I	N	A

All these pets are rodents, apart from the rabbit, which is a lagomorph. Read the next section to find out the difference!

Design a pet playground

Mr Brisbane gave me the BEST Christmas gift ever when he presented me with my very own hamster playground. It has a tiny seesaw, a tree branch and two ladders (one is like a bridge). I always love playing in it!

If you could design a playground for your pet, what would you have in it? Think about the kind of playgrounds that you like. Which kind would your pet find the most fun?

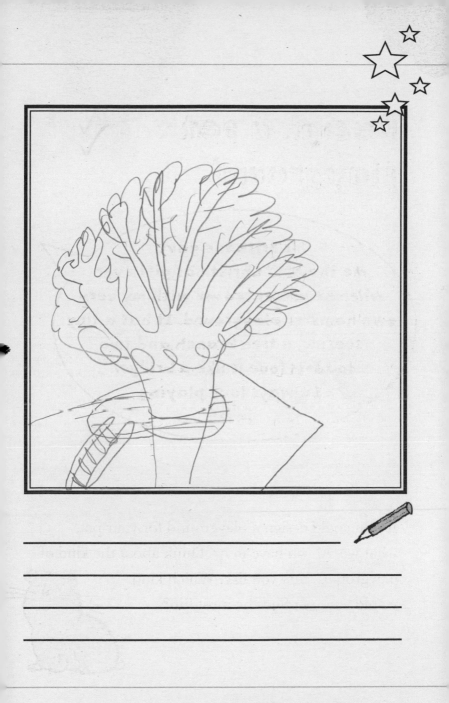

_____

_____

_____

_____

Rodent shadow match

Look carefully at these five rodent pets. Can you match them to their shadows? Draw lines between the two.

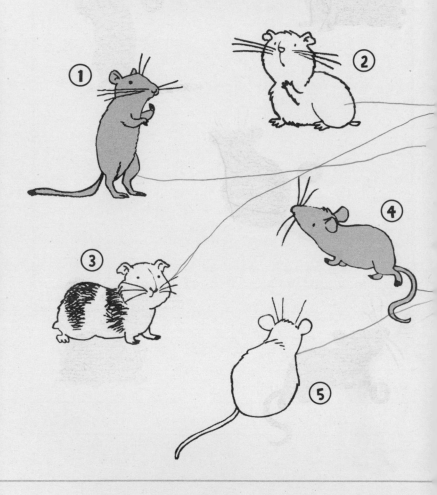

CUDDLY RABBITS

Rabbits are intelligent, inquisitive and energetic – as well as being the most strokeable pets because of their super-soft fur. Known for their incredibly long floppy ears, rabbits have excellent hearing and can even move their ears around to listen out for particular sounds. This is very important, as in the wild, rabbits are preyed on by other animals and they need to be constantly on the lookout for enemies. An excellent sense of smell, and the ability to see almost 360° around themselves helps the rabbit to avoid dangerous situations. And when they detect danger, rabbits thump their strong hind legs to warn their rabbit friends.

When I detect danger, I SQUEAK-SQUEAK-SQUEAK as loudly as I can!

Boo!

I love little hiding places too. Hide and SQUEAK is one of my favourite games!

A hutch is home

Space is really important for rabbits and not all hutches sold in pet shops are big enough. A rabbit hutch should be large enough to allow the rabbit to stretch out fully in all directions, high enough for the rabbit to stand up fully on its back legs, and long enough to allow the rabbit to hop forward a few times. The hutch needs to have a place where the rabbit can comfortably sleep and also a place where she can hide away when she wants to. This is very important to rabbits.

Rabbits need lots of exercise so will also need a run to hop around in. Make sure that your rabbit gets plenty of exercise time outside the hutch every day.

As rabbits are often kept outside, the hutch will need to be positioned away from direct sunlight and draughts. It should also be raised off the ground, which can be done with bricks. If it gets very cold in the winter, the hutch may have to be moved inside or into a garage.

!

Important: Your rabbit's hutch and run must be made escape-proof and kept safe from potential predators such as dogs, cats, foxes and rats.

Some creatures can be harmful to smaller pets, so you need to take special care of us. THANKS-THANKS-THANKS!

The hutch should be lined with newspaper or wood shavings, with soft hay or straw on top. Make sure your rabbit has lots of clean, dry hay or straw in its sleeping area for a cosy bed. The hutch should also have a separate place where the rabbit can go to the toilet away from her eating and sleeping areas.

Clean the hutch every day by removing any dirty or wet straw and uneaten fresh food. Once a week you'll need to give the hutch a proper clean-out with special pet detergent and replace all the hay and grass.

Feeding your rabbit

Rabbits are herbivores, which means they only eat plants. They need to eat lots of good-quality hay and grass (an amount equal to their own body size every day is a good guide). You can also give them some shop-bought rabbit pellets and they will enjoy a small amount of fresh vegetables a couple of times a day. Broccoli, cabbage, green beans and the leafy tops of carrots (but only a small amount of the orange part as this is high in sugar) are all good snacks.

Make sure your pet has plenty of clean water every day. A special water bottle with a metal spout is a good way to provide this.

I have a special drinking bottle just like this! It's UNSQUEAKABLY great to have water on tap.

Did you know that some plants are poisonous to rabbits, including oak leaves, evergreens, rhubarb leaves and anything that grows from a bulb? There are many others, so don't let your rabbit go near plants or flowerbeds if you are not sure whether they might contain poisonous plants.

Behaviour and play

Rabbits are sociable creatures and enjoy the company of other rabbits. It is best to keep rabbits in pairs – a neutered (see page 92) male and female pair usually makes a good combination but ask your vet for advice. If a rabbit is left on its own for too long she will become very lonely, so make sure you spend plenty of time playing with and keeping your rabbit company every day. You should also get your rabbit used to being handled from a young age so that she doesn't get too nervous about being held and stroked.

Follow this advice and your rabbit won't be 'UN-HOPPY'!

It's a good idea to give your rabbit some safe toys to play with. Toys for rabbits are available from pet shops and include things like large tubes and platforms to climb onto. Cardboard boxes and safe, untreated logs are also good for rabbits to explore. Rabbits need to chew a lot to keep their teeth healthy, so you can allow them to chew on untreated wooden blocks, balls and paper toilet rolls.

You'll find that your pet rabbit is at her most active in the morning and late afternoon. In the wild, rabbits emerge from their burrows at dawn and dusk, although in warm sunny weather you might spot a wild rabbit out during the day.

Protection and care

As rabbits are prey for many creatures in the wild, hiding places are very important to them. Even pet rabbits need somewhere to hide away when they are in their hutch and when playing in their run as rabbits can get very frightened if they feel that they are exposed.

They are usually very scared of cats and dogs and in most cases it is best to keep them apart. Signs that your rabbit may be suffering from stress can include hiding, chewing cage bars, a sudden change in feeding or toilet habits, sitting hunched, not wanting to move, and constantly circling her enclosure.

I understand how it feels to be frightened. Other animals can just seem so big and SCARY. When Clem the dog first bounded up to my cage and stuck his nose against the bars, I was shaking and quaking!

Rabbit health

Take your rabbit for a routine health check with your vet once each year and check her front teeth and nails once a week, as these can grow quickly. Rabbits are especially prone to dental problems and can get eye discharges when they have trouble with their teeth, so keep a lookout for this. The most important thing you can do for your rabbit is to feed her the right diet and check her teeth regularly. Do not feed her rabbit mixes from the pet shop (they look like muesli) as rabbits need mainly grass and hay to eat.

If you're worried about losing your rabbit, you can get a microchip inserted into your pet just as you can with cats and dogs.

It's a very good idea to get your rabbit neutered, especially if you have more than one.

What is neutering?

This is an operation carried out by a vet. It is quite usual and thousands of pets have it done to them every year. In male animals, the testicles are removed, while in female animals, the ovaries and the uterus are taken out. The pet is put to sleep so that it doesn't feel anything. Afterwards, they will not be able to have babies. As there are so many unwanted animals around, most people agree that it's better not to add to the numbers.

Vets will usually recommend neutering as it can help your pet avoid some diseases and live a longer, healthier life. It can also improve behaviour and make it less likely that your pet will have an accident. There is nothing to worry about – your pet won't suffer and it is a very safe operation.

Rabbit facts

✱ Rabbits are fast! They have powerful hind legs and can sometimes reach speeds of up to 50 miles (about 80km) an hour!

✱ Wild rabbits dig underground tunnels called burrows. This network of inter-connecting burrows is called a 'warren'. Fifty or more rabbits can live in one warren.

✱ Rabbits belong to a group of mammals called lagomorphs. Like rodents, lagomorphs have incisor (front) teeth that keep growing. The difference is that lagomorphs have two pairs of incisors in their upper jaw while rodents have just one pair.

✱ Pet rabbits can be trained to come when they are called and can even be taught to use a litter tray as their toilet.

✽ Rabbits can sometimes make a 'purring' sound that is similar to that made by a cat.

✽ Rabbits eat some of their droppings! A rabbit produces two different types of droppings – hard, dry ones, and dark smelly ones. The second type are special ones called 'caecotrophs' and rabbits eat them in order to get as much goodness as possible from their food. It's perfectly normal behaviour for a rabbit.

I thought Og eating live crickets was disgusting but eating your poo – that's got to be the WORST!

JOKING AROUND WITH HUMPHREY

I'd like to hear a rabbit tell a joke. That would be a *FUNNY* bunny!

Q. How can you tell which rabbits are the oldest in a group?

A. Look for the grey hares.

Q. A bumblebee started chasing a rabbit. Then the bee changed his mind and buzzed off. Why?

A. The rabbit had two 'b's already!

Q. What do rabbits sing once a year?
A. 'Hoppy birthday to you...'

Q. Why did the rabbit build herself a new house?
A. She was fed up with the hole thing!

Q. What is the difference between a crazy bunny and a fake banknote?
A. One is bad money and the other is a mad bunny.

Q. Why did the rabbit bang his head on the piano?
A. She was playing by ear.

Q. What do you get if you cross a frog and a rabbit?
A. A rabbit that says 'ribbit'.

Q. What do you call a dumb bunny?
A. A hare brain.

HUMPHREY'S RABBIT FUN

Rabbit word challenge

How many words can you make out of the word **RABBITS** I've written one down to start you off!

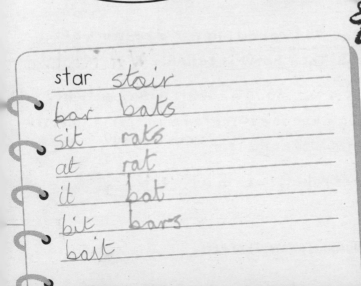

star · stair
bar · bats
sit · rats
at · rat
it · bat
bit · bars
bait

Bunny brainpower crossword

Are you a bunny brainbox? Find out how much you know about rabbits with this 'FURRY' tricky crossword!

CLUES

DOWN

1. In the wild, rabbits live in a network of burrows. Their home is called a <u>WARREN</u>

3. This is the sound a rabbit makes with her hind leg when she is scared and trying to warn other rabbits of danger.

5. A pet rabbit lives in a <u>hutch</u>

ACROSS

2. It's easy to identify a rabbit because of her long _E A R S_

4. What a rabbit is covered with.

5. This is what a rabbit does when she is scared and doesn't want to be seen.

6. A rabbit is a herbivore and only eats _p l a n t s_

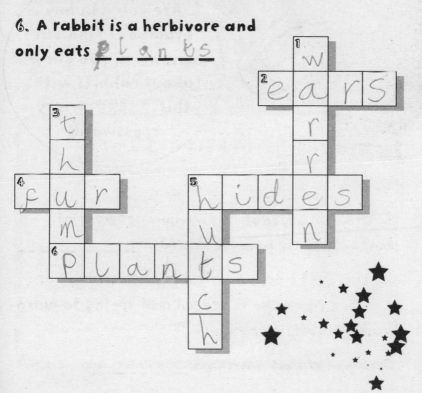

Finish the rabbit

Can you complete this long-eared picture by joining the dots? Then draw the rabbit's eyes and add some LOVELY long whiskers!

!

EAR'S AN INTERESTING THING!
The longest rabbit ears measured an incredible 79cm from top to bottom (that's about 31 inches). They belonged to a rabbit called Nipper's Geronimo and they were measured at a rabbit show in Kansas, USA, on 1 November 2003. Nipper's ears were so long that they flopped down on to the ground!

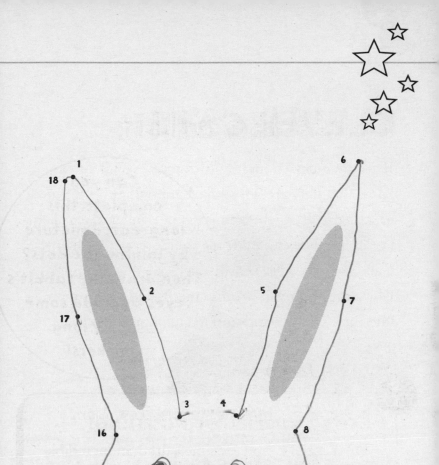

CLEVER CATS

If you're lucky enough to own a cat, you'll already know that they are very smart animals. They have a great sense of smell, very good hearing and excellent eyesight – they can even see well in very dim light. Cats also have very sensitive whiskers, which pick up vibrations in the air around them. This helps them to find their way around and to catch prey.

PREY? **Now that makes me nervous. I once found myself trapped in the paws of a cat in a garden. Thank goodness I was in my hamster ball at the time. Otherwise I might have found myself in hamster heaven!**

It's my territory!

Cats are territorial creatures. This means that they like to have their own space – and they will defend this space against a rival or unknown cat. Cats identify their territory by 'marking' it. A cat might do a wee or a poo or scratch around a certain area to show that it's hers. Cats also produce scent from glands on their heads and paws and will rub themselves against an object to leave their scent behind. Because cats have a super-strong sense of smell they can easily sniff out their own scent or that of another creature. So when a cat rubs up against you in a friendly way, she is passing her scent onto you and joining you into her personal 'club'!

Cat safety

Cats, especially kittens, are very playful and will love jumping up and patting things with their paws or try to 'catch' objects that are dangling. They are great fun to watch. But look out for electrical wires and tablecloths which your pet could easily bring crashing down. Put away anything sharp that could hurt your cat, as well as plastic bags and bottles of detergent and cleaning fluids, which could injure her.

As a pet owner, it's up to you to avoid a CAT-astrophe!

Kittens, in particular, need special care because they love to explore and don't have much sense of danger. Gates and doors leading out onto the road should be kept closed and any small holes in the floorboards blocked or covered up. A small kitten can find her way into a surprising number of places, so try to look around your house from a kitten's point of view and make sure it is safe before your pet arrives.

If you have a new cat or kitten coming to the house you should stay close by for the first few hours to keep it company. This shouldn't be too hard – your kitten will be so cute you probably won't be able to leave her alone! Give your cat time to get used to you and her new home and perhaps keep her in just one or two rooms for the first few days – it can all be a bit overwhelming otherwise. Make a comfy bed for your cat using a basket or a box lined with cushions or blankets.

Everyone needs time to get used to new places. Room 26 of Longfellow School seemed very different from being in the pet shop and I felt strange for the first few days. But now it's my FAVOURITE place in the whole world.

How does your cat feel?

It's usually easy to tell how your cat is feeling because of her body language. Purring, rubbing up against you and generally looking happy are all good signs. Hissing, ears back or flattened, arching her back and waving her tail around a lot will mean she is unhappy or angry.

One thing that makes most cats happy is being stroked. Remember that you should always stroke from the head downwards to the tail. Cats don't generally like being stroked in the other direction. They don't usually like their tails being touched either. But your cat will probably love being gently scratched on her head and just behind the ears. Purr!

I agree.
Being stroked and petted is just so NICE-NICE-NICE!
If I could purr,
I would!

Things NOT to do to your cat

* Never feed your cat human treats like sweets but, most importantly, never give your cat chocolate. It's a treat for us, but poisonous to cats and it can make them very sick. Chocolate is also toxic to horses, dogs and parrots.

* Don't feed your cat chicken bones or fish with bones in it, as she could choke on them.

✻ Never pick up your cat by the scruff of her neck. Cats do pick up their own kittens by the scruffs of their necks when they are very small but humans may hurt a cat if they try to do this.

✻ Don't squeeze your cat. As with all pets, be gentle. The best way to pick up a cat is to use both arms to gently hold and support her by her chest and back legs. If you have a cat that likes being cuddled you can bring her close to your body and have a gentle hug.

No one likes being squeezed really tightly. I'm so LUCKY as all my friends in Room 26 are very gentle with me.

Grooming

Cats use their rough tongues and sharp teeth to groom themselves very effectively. In fact, cats spend almost 30% of their lives grooming themselves! However, cats still benefit from being brushed, especially if your pet is a longhaired cat. To do this you will need a special cat brush from a pet shop. Like stroking, always brush from the head to the tail. Look out for fleas (tiny dark insects) and, if you find any, get advice on how to get rid of them from your pet shop or vet.

I'm a GREAT groomer too! But no one needs to brush me — I do a pretty good job all by myself.

Feeding your cat

Cats need a meat-based diet to stay healthy. Kittens generally need three small meals a day and adult cats need to eat once or twice a day. They can eat dry cat food or tinned cat food, or fresh cooked chicken and fish (but no bones!). Always make sure your cat has got enough water in her bowl as she needs to drink regularly.

Cat training

Cats use litter boxes in the same way that people use toilets. But they need to learn first of all. Young cats need toilet training and, just like humans, they like to be praised when they have done something right.

So when your cat is learning to do a poo or wee in the litter tray, make sure that you stroke and praise her whenever the job is done well! It's also important that their 'toilet' is kept clean. A grown-up will need to do this, scooping the poo out every day and completely changing the litter once a month.

> Yes, I've noticed that teachers like Ms Mac and Mrs Brisbane always praise the students when they've done something well. This REALLY seems to work!

Cats are very intelligent creatures and can be trained to do lots of things, such as coming when they're called. As before, it's all about giving praise and rewards. If you call your cat's name every time you feed her, this will teach her that the word means food is coming and she should come running up to you. However, if your cat does something you don't want her to do (like scratching the furniture) say 'No' firmly (but never shout) and gently move the cat away. Offer the cat an alternative, like a scratching post, as she needs to test her claws out. If your cat doesn't respond, you could try clapping your hands as well as saying 'No'. Cats hate sudden noises!

Playtime!

Cats love to play and you'll have a great time being their playmate. Boxes with holes cut in them, scrunched-up newspaper balls, straws and pieces of wool or string are all good cat toys.

Play lots of games – try rolling a ball for your cat across the floor (there are special noisy balls that you can buy from pet shops) but make sure the ball isn't so small that it can be swallowed by your pet. Another really enjoyable game is to tie a feather on to a stick with a length of string or wool. You can then dangle the pretend 'fish' in front of your cat, who will enjoy trying to catch it. Make sure that you let her actually get hold of the 'fish' from time to time. You can also use the feather and string for a great pouncing game by letting the feather slide and dance across the floor in front of your cat.

These games sound FABULOUS. I wouldn't mind trying one or two myself!

Your cat needs to have exercise each day to stay fit. If she doesn't go outside much, make sure you have some indoor activities to keep your cat busy. Many cats enjoy climbing and you can buy special 'cat trees' from pet shops, which are a kind of climbing frame for cats.

Cat health

When you first get a cat, you will need to take her to the vet to make sure she is healthy. Ask your vet for advice about things you can do to protect your cat's health, such as vaccination, neutering (see page 92) and treatments to control fleas and worms. Be observant. If your cat's behaviour suddenly changes or if she shows signs of stress or fear, seek advice from a vet.

It's also a good idea to get your cat kitted out with a clever little device called a microchip, which will help you find her if she gets lost. This is a tiny little computer chip which is inserted under the cat's skin (don't worry, it doesn't hurt). If your pet is found, a vet can read the chip with a special scanner, which will bring up the owner's details.

Cat facts

* Cats were very important to the Ancient Egyptians. They kept them as pets and also associated them with their gods. The Egyptians believed that the cat was the special animal of the goddess Bastet. They would sometimes leave the goddess a gift of a mummified cat to please her.

* Did you think cats don't like water? Well, think again! There is a cat called the Bengali Mach-Bagral, which is found in Nepal and parts of India and China. She is known as the swimming cat because she swims to catch fish! She has extra long claws which she uses like fishhooks to spear the fish.

* Cats don't just 'meow'. They communicate with a whole range of different noises – purrs, growls, 'chirrups', yowls and hisses.

✳ Cats sleep a lot – usually about 12–18 hours a day.

Zzzzz

Now that's something cats and I have in common — we just LOVE our catnaps!

✳ All cat owners will know that cats sometimes bring dead mice and birds into the house. This is because cats are natural hunters. Once they've killed their prey, they will often leave it for you as a present. It may not be your idea of a gift but it's your cat's way of being generous!

✳ Cats often make 'kneading' motions with their paws, on to an object or perhaps onto your lap (which can be a bit painful!). Your cat is remembering when she was a kitten and she used to knead her mother's tummy to ask her for milk.

JOKING AROUND WITH HUMPHREY

I think you'll find these jokes PURR-FECT for a good laugh!

Q. Did you hear the one about the cat who swallowed a ball of wool?
A. She had mittens!

Q. How do you know when your cat has been using your computer?
A. When there are teethmarks on the mouse.

Q. What do you get if you cross a hungry cat and a canary?
A. A cat that isn't hungry any more.

Q. How does a cat start a race?
A. One, mew, three!

Q. What kind of cat keeps the grass short?
A. A lawn meower.

Q. Why are cats longer in the evening than they are in the morning?
A. Because they are let out in the evening and taken in, in the morning.

Q. Which cat purrs more than any other?
A. A purr-sian.

Q. How do you spell mouse-trap in just three letters?
A. C-A-T!

HUMPHREY'S CAT FUN
Cat know-how

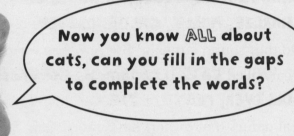

Now you know ALL about cats, can you fill in the gaps to complete the words?

Things you often see cats doing

1. Sl e e ping
2. Sc r a tching
3. G r ooming

Parts of a cat's body

4. C l a ws
5. Wh i s kers
6. T ail

Noises cats make

7. M eow
8. Pu r r
9. H i ss

What's in a name?

What do you think the most popular cat names are?
Here are a few of the most common names around.
**MAX, TIGGER, TIGER, SMUDGE, SMOKEY,
CHARLIE, MOLLY, CHLOE, OLIVER.**
Do they sound familiar? But have you ever heard of
a cat called **CATZILLA, BASIL, SNICKLEFRITZ,
GULLIVER, PESTO** or **THE COUNT**? These are all
real names that owners have called their cats!

What would be your favourite name for a cat or kitten?

KITTY

When I stayed at
Garth's house for the
weekend I met a cat called
'Sweetums'. Unfortunately,
she was NOTHING like
her name!

Cat word grid

I'm not a big fan of cats but I do know that they are VERY clever. Are you as clever as a cat? Solve the clues going across to find another cat-related word in the down box.

CLUES

1. What cats do with their tongues, especially when grooming themselves.

2. Cats like to eat this. It can be a bit smelly!

3. If a cat gets annoyed, you might see this part of her body waving around

1. LICK
2. FISH
3. TAIL
4. HUNT
5. FLEA
6. NAP

4. Cats often chase mice and birds because they like to H U N T

5. Watch out for this irritating insect — it likes to live in a cat's fur.

6. Sleep is very important to cats and you'll often see them having one of these during the day.

DASHING DOGS

It's no surprise that dogs are one of the most popular pets around. They're intelligent, loyal and make fantastic playmates. They are also very faithful companions. If you have a dog, you've got a friend for life. And there are so many different breeds and varieties of dog to choose from, from tiny terriers and cute little lapdogs to huge hairy hounds and shaggy sheepdogs!

Hmm. I'm not sure if I could ever really be friends with a dog. Dogs may be 'Man's Best Friend' but they're certainly NOT a 'Hamster's Best Friend'.

Understanding your dog

Dogs are great communicators and can tell you almost instantly if they're happy and joyful or just feeling downright grumpy. They do this through body language — facial expressions and ear and body movements, especially their tails. An energetically wagging tail is one of the easiest ways to know if a dog is happy. Dog experts have also worked out that dogs have about a hundred different facial expressions!

Dogs also make an amazing range of sounds, from barks and deep growls to high-pitched whimpers and yaps. These sounds help us understand what it is they want and whether they are happy or sad.

Oh yes, I knew right away that Miranda's dog, Clem, wanted to EAT me. I could tell by his huge lolling tongue and the hungry look in his eyes!

Scent is extremely important to dogs as they have a highly developed sense of smell. You're sure to have noticed that dogs sniff each other when they are first meeting. It's their way of saying 'hello'. You will also have noticed that dogs seem to enjoying lifting their legs and peeing on trees and lamp posts. Why do they do this? Your dog uses smell to help identify and recognise other dogs. Dogs also leave their scent behind where other dogs will smell it. This is because they are territorial – they like to mark their space or 'territory' to other dogs. A dog will lift its back legs to pee on the side of a tree as high as it possibly can so that it will seem as if a really big dog has been there before!

Walkies!

Dogs need *lots* of exercise and must run around every day. Taking your dog for a good walk twice a day (most people go early morning and in the evening) will give you and your family plenty of exercise as well. It also provides an opportunity for your dog to go to the toilet. But make sure someone picks up the poop afterwards! There are various pooper scooper gadgets around, but it's quite simple to do it with a couple of small plastic (ideally biodegradable) bags, putting one over your hand and using one as the poop bag. When you've 'scooped that poop' make sure you dispose of it in a special poop bin.

Keep your dog on a lead when out for a walk, and only take the lead off when you are absolutely sure it is safe. This protects your dog from traffic as well as making sure that your pet isn't being a nuisance to other people. Try to find a park with a large area that dogs are welcome to run around in.

Clem has a LOT-LOT-LOT of energy and really needs to run it off. Luckily he has a lovely owner — Miranda — who takes him for lots of walks in the park.

In many countries, dog owners will need to buy a licence for their dog and their pets may need to wear a collar with their owner's name and address clearly marked, or on an attached tag. You will need to check what the rules are wherever you live. Dogs can also be fitted with a microchip, which will help them to be identified if they are ever lost. This is really worthwhile.

If your dog is getting enough exercise during the day, he should sleep well at night. Make him a nice cosy bed in a quiet, draught-free area. Dog baskets or large boxes lined with old cushions and blankets work well.

Important: You are responsible for your dog and must keep him under control in public places like parks. Some dogs like to chase other animals – and people! So don't let your dog off the lead until you are confident that he won't cause chaos. And if he does, get him back on to the lead as quickly as possible.

Playtime

Dogs love to play. They will usually tell you that they want to play with you by crouching down on their front legs while their back legs are still standing. The eager, expectant expression on their faces will clearly let you know that it's playtime. Dogs will love it if you throw a ball, a stick or a flying disc for them and will eagerly fetch it back, begging you to throw it again.

Another good game you can play is hide and seek. Hide somewhere away from your dog, then call him to you. If he can't find you, keep on calling. As he gets used to the game, make it more difficult for him to find you. You can also have a doggy 'treasure hunt' by hiding treats in different places while your dog waits. At the command of 'Go!' he runs around, searching out and finding all the treats.

Hide the Treat is a REALLY fun game that can be played with all kinds of pets — hamsters too!

Dogs are very sociable animals who usually like company, whether it be human or dog. They will be unhappy if they are left alone for long periods of time. So make sure that your dog has lots of opportunities to play with and interact with other humans and dogs. You should do this from a young age, if possible, as the more a young dog experiences other people and everyday sights and sounds, the more sociable and friendly he will be as an adult dog.

Having a friend is SO important, whether it's a human one or an animal one. I'm so lucky to have lots of both!

Chew on this!

Dogs love to bite and chew on things and they need to do this to keep their teeth and jaws healthy. Young dogs in particular will probably try and chew everything in sight as they test things out and discover their surroundings. Help them by providing lots of things that are safe and tough enough to survive being chewed. There are special chews to buy at most pet shops that are made out of hide and come in all kinds of different shapes. There are also chewy toys you can buy. It's a good idea to teach your dog what is and isn't acceptable to chew around the house.

Yes, I heard that a dog's favourite day is CHEWSDAY!

> Practice — and patience — always pay off. TREATS are good too!

Training

Dogs are highly intelligent creatures and they learn very quickly. They can be trained to come when they're called, to 'Sit' on a command, to fetch things for you and to do tricks, like rolling on their backs. The key to successful training is to make it fun! Give clear commands and give your dog lots of praise when he does the right thing. Dogs respond really well to praise and rewards when you are trying to teach them something new. But don't expect your training to work the very first time – practice makes perfect. Regular, short sessions work best so that no one gets bored. Never punish your dog or shout at him.

Toilet training

All dogs need to be housetrained – taught that they must go to the toilet outside. Young puppies will be very messy to start off with and you and your family will probably find yourselves doing a lot of cleaning up. You need to help your pet by showing him the place where you want him to go and giving him lots of praise when he wees or poos in the right area. Take your puppy outside for this purpose at least every two hours, after eating or drinking, and especially after playing. In time, and with lots of practice, he will be letting you know it is time for him to go out to the toilet. Always give your dog lots of praise for a job well done and try to take him out around the same time every day so that he will get used to going to the toilet at this time.

(It's really useful to get your dog into a routine as much as possible. It will help him feel secure and understand what is expected of him. Being fed, exercised and going to the toilet at a similar time every day will make it all much easier for you and your pet.)

Food for dogs

Dogs need to eat a balanced diet that will keep them healthy but also one that will not make them overweight. As dogs vary enormously in size, they will need a different amount of food depending on their weight. From the age of about five weeks, puppies need about four meals a day, going down to three meals at about three months of age. At six months old, they can be fed twice a day, which is the usual for an adult dog.

There are many different brands of dog food on the market for different stages of a dog's life and you will soon find out which your pet prefers. Remember to throw out any uneaten food after your dog has finished his meal.

Never give your dog chocolate, onions, grapes or raisins, as these are poisonous to dogs. You can buy special dog treats from the pet shop if you want to give your pet an occasional reward, but he is better off with a healthy snack such as a piece of apple or carrot.

YUM. Apple and carrot are my favourites too! They're delicious and great for chewing on.

You will need to provide your dog with lots of clean drinking water in a bowl.

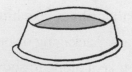

A healthy dog

When you first get your dog, you should take him to the vet for a check-up and ask for advice about things you can do to protect your pet's health, such as vaccination, neutering (see page 92), and treatments for fleas and worms. Following this, you should take your pet for a routine check-up once a year.

A healthy dog is fit and energetic, has bright eyes and a wet nose. If your dog seems unwell or his usual behaviour changes, get him checked to see if there is something wrong.

As dogs have a tendency to nibble on things left lying around, vets do sometimes see dogs that have been poisoned. Sometimes dogs eat poison which has been left out for rats or mice, or they eat medicines that are meant for humans. If you think your pet might have eaten something bad for him, take him immediately to the vet. If there is any packaging or other clue as to what the dog has eaten, take it along to show the vet too.

Dog facts

* Dogs are descended from wolves. Experts think that humans living thousands of years ago first tamed wolves to live alongside them.

* Dogs have an amazing sense of smell. Humans have about 5 million smell-detecting cells, cats have about 100 million and dogs have up to 220 million cells! Dogs can be trained to sniff out all kinds of things that humans wouldn't have a hope of finding with our noses. In the military, dogs can be trained to sniff out explosives and weapons. Some highly trained dogs are even able to detect diseases in humans.

* Dogs are incredibly helpful to humans. Different breeds of dog can work as guards, hunters, eyes for the blind (guide dogs) and as searchers for missing people.

* 'Max' is the most popular name for dogs in the U.S., U.K. and Australia.

✱ A dog's nose 'print' is as individual as a human's fingerprints. Every dog has a unique pattern of ridges and dimples, which, along with his nostril shape, make up his own personal nose print.

✱ Many breeds of dog can run really fast but the greyhound is probably the fastest dog in the world. He has been known to reach speeds of almost 45mph.

You know,
I can spin pretty fast in
my hamster wheel but I'm
not sure I can spin
THAT fast!

JOKING AROUND WITH HUMPHREY

Q. What is the dogs' favourite city?
A. New yorkie.

Q. What dog can jump higher than a tree?
A. Any dog can jump higher than a tree. Trees can't jump.

HEY!
That means I can jump higher than a tree, too!

Q. What do dogs eat at the cinema?
A. Pup-corn.

Q. What's a dog's favourite food?
A. Anything that's on your plate.

Q. What do you call a small, scared dog?
A. Terrier-fied!

Q. What kind of dogs are best with kids?
A. Baby setters.

Q. When do dogs have 16 legs?
A. When there are four of them.

Q. How is a dog lying down like a coin?
A. Because he has his head on one side and his tail on the other.

HUMPHREY'S DOG FUN
Doggy wordsnake

> **Look at all these different kinds of dog — I never knew there were SO many!**

Can you find the dogs in the grid opposite? Use a pencil to draw a continuous line through the words, which 'snake' around, up and down, backwards and forwards, but never diagonally. The words are in the same order as the list below.

TERRIER • POODLE • COLLIE • HUSKY
SPANIEL • DALMATIAN • BULLDOG
LABRADOR • BOXER

Find

T	E	R	X	E	R
E	I	R	O	B	R
R	P	O	O	D	O
C	E	L	D	A	R
O	L	L	O	G	B
S	U	I	D	L	A
K	H	E	L	L	U
Y	I	E	A	N	B
S	N	L	I	T	A
P	A	D	A	L	M

Design a dog toy

I've seen lots of dogs running around after balls and they really seem to LOVE playing with them. But can you design a completely new kind of toy for a dog? Remember, dogs enjoy chewing, catching, fetching, running and looking for things.

NEW BOMB-BALL

Doggy noises

When the kids at Longfellow School talk about dogs, they say 'WOOF WOOF!'. But how do dogs bark around the world?

Mandarin Chinese: WANG WANG

Balinese: KONG KONG

Albanian: HAM HAM

Italian: BAU BAU

Indonesian: GUK GUK

Swedish: VOFF VOFF

Turkish: HEV HEV

Urdu: BOW BOW

Which one do you think best describes a dog's bark?

FASCINATING FISH

Owning a fish is a very different kind of experience. Unlike many other pets, you can't pick them up and give them a cuddle! But fish certainly have their own unique appeal. They can be absolutely beautiful to look at and they are very relaxing to watch as they swim around their tank. Fish come in an incredible variety of shapes, colours and patterns and make a great choice if you're fascinated by all things aquatic. It's also great fun to create an underwater environment for your own fish.

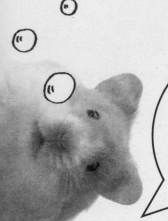

I LOVED seeing the aquarium at the vet's surgery. It was filled with fish of every colour. Some had stripes, others polka dots and they were swimming around a pink castle!

Which kind of fish?

There are two main types of fish that are kept as pets – coldwater fish and tropical freshwater fish. Like their name, the first type live in – you've guessed it – *cold* water! Goldfish are the most popular type of fish in this category and they are ideal pets for a first-time fish owner. Tropical freshwater fish need warm water to live in so they need a specially heated tank.

Types of goldfish

Choosing a goldfish can be quite difficult as there are more than a hundred varieties! Some have beautiful floating tails, others have unusually shaped heads, swirly patterns or glittering scales. There are also some great and unusual names for different types of goldfish. How about a Comet or perhaps a Pom Pom, Telescope Eye, Fantail, Panda Moor, Shubunkin or Lionhead?

WOW! Some of these fish sound really interesting. I wonder if the Lionhead really looks like a lion?

Roaarrr!

The right tank

You will need to get as big a tank as possible – the old-fashioned round type of goldfish bowl is definitely too small and not at all suitable for keeping fish in. Ask for some advice from your pet shop on the kind of tank to buy but, generally speaking, the fish tank will be made from glass or plastic, have a lid and an electric pump and filter to keep the water clean. It will probably have lights – these should be turned on during the day and switched off at night. A good-sized fish tank, plus all the extras you will need (not forgetting the fish!) can be quite expensive.

You'll need special gravel to put on the floor of the tank, a small net, a cleaning kit and a thermometer to check the water temperature.

Fishy fun

Once you've got the basics together you can start creating a great environment for your fishy friend. Add lots of plants and make an aquatic 'forest' – this not only looks good, but will keep your fish healthy as the plants put oxygen into the water. You will be able to buy the right kind of aquatic plants from the pet shop. Construct hidey-holes and caves using different-sized rocks and pebbles and perhaps decorate the tank with shells. Maybe even 'splash out' on some special tank ornaments from the pet shop. You can get all sorts of fun things such as pirate ships, castles, bridges and 'opening' treasure chests!

Wouldn't it be great to have a PIRATE ship in your aquarium? I hear fish and ships are a good combination!

Make sure you only decorate the tank with things specially selected for aquariums, as rocks and shells taken from the beach may be polluted.

The aquarium in the school library has a tiny BOAT lying at the bottom of it — I often wonder what must have happened to make it sink?

SS GOLDEN HAMSTER

Bear in mind that you cannot buy a fish and a tank on the same day as there is a lot of preparation required. Buy the tank a week or more *before* you get the fish to give you time to prepare everything. The water you put in the tank will need to be de-chlorinated first. Tap water contains a chemical called chlorine, which is really bad for fish.

You can put special drops or tablets into the water to get rid of the chlorine or leave the water to stand in a bucket for 24 hours, to let the chlorine escape. An adult will need to help you to follow the instructions on the tank and fit the water filter and the light. Don't put lots of fish into your tank at once – just one or two at a time to let them settle in. How many fish you can have will depend on how large your tank is and the size and the type of fish you choose.

Important: Place your tank on a firm surface or buy a good solid stand for it. Keep it away from direct sunlight and radiators/heaters.

Remember – a goldfish is a COLD water fish and needs to stay that way!

Looking after tropical fish

Owning and setting up a tropical freshwater fish takes a little more time than with coldwater fish. You'll need to set up a heated tank and check and maintain the water temperature at a constant 24°C. As well as all the items you need for a coldwater fish, you'll also need a special heater and a thermostat, which your pet shop can advise you on. But once you have done all the preparation, your reward will be the choice of fish. There are some incredible varieties of tropical freshwater fish: stripy orange clownfish (like Nemo), luminous neon tetras, colourful rainbow fish, floaty angelfish … the choice seems endless.

If your tank (and your wallet) is big enough to buy several fish, try selecting types that like living at different levels of the tank. Like their name, surface feeders (e.g. glass catfish) enjoy being at the top of the tank, while bottom feeders (e.g. the clown loach) are useful as they suck food from the bottom of the tank and help keep it clean. There are also fish that like being in the middle of the tank. (e.g. tetras and angelfish). Your pet shop will be able to help you identify each type.

Taking it home

Whichever fish you decide on, it will probably be put into a plastic bag for you to take it home in. Float the bag on the tank water for about half an hour so that the temperature of the water inside the bag adjusts to that of the water outside. Then open the bag and let a little of the tank water inside. Finally, allow the fish to swim out of the container into the new tank. **NEVER** tip the fish directly into the water – be gentle!

> **Important:**
> ✳ A sudden change of temperature will shock your fish and it could even die.
> ✳ Never touch your fish with your hands – always use a net.

Feeding

It's tempting to give your fish lots of food but beware – fish can easily die if they are over-fed. Too much food will also make the water dirty. Follow the instructions carefully on your fish-food container. Most food is scattered on the surface of the water.

It's a shame that fish don't have handy pouches in their cheeks, like ME! Then they could save some tasty snacks for later.

Even if it seems a small amount, do not add any extra food or feed the fish more often than the directions state. Your fish will soon learn when food is arriving and will quickly swim towards the surface when you scatter it. Wait ten minutes or so then skim off any uneaten food.

Cleaning the tank

Cleaning the tank out may not be the most fun job but it is a very important one. Your fish breathes in this water so it needs to be clean for your pet to stay healthy. Once every two weeks you will need to replace some of the old water with clean de-chlorinated water. First, you'll need an adult to help remove about a third of the water into a bucket with a siphon. Use the net to gently take your fish out and put it into this bucket while you clean the tank. Scrape off any slime from the walls and remove any dead plant material or food. Put the fish back in the tank, then, little by little, replace the water with the clean water. Check the filter and clean or replace if necessary.

Fish health

Try to make sure that the fish you choose are as healthy as possible. Always choose an active fish with smooth scales (look out for white spots, not a good sign). Check that the fish is swimming properly, not tilting to one side, and that its fins are straight and not floppy.

The best way to keep your fish healthy is to make sure the tank is kept clean and that you are not over-feeding him. Sometimes fish get diseases, such as white spot, which is a tiny parasite. There are quite a few treatments that you can buy from pet shops for various fish problems. If you have several fish and just one is sick, it's a good idea to put him in a separate 'recovery' tank for a while so that the other fish don't get sick as well.

Fishy facts

✳ Some goldfish have been known to live for over 40 years.

✳ Goldfish originated from a species of fish called the Crucian carp. It is believed that they were first kept as pets in China around AD 800.

✳ Fish don't sleep like humans and other animals do. This is because fish don't have any eyelids so it's impossible for them to shut their eyes! But they do rest with their eyes open.

Impossible to shut their eyes? That sounds AWFUL. I really prefer to sleep with my eyes closed.

✳ A baby fish is called a 'fry'. And a pregnant goldfish is called a 'twit'!

✳ There are more known species of fish than all the species of amphibians, reptiles, birds and mammals combined.

JOKING AROUND WITH HUMPHREY

I won't keep all these jokes to myself — that would be SHELLFISH!

Q. Why is it so easy to weigh fish?
A. Because they have their own scales.

Q. What do you get when you cross a fish with a herd of elephants?
A. Swimming trunks.

Q. What kind of fish are useful in icy weather?
A. Skates.

Q. Why couldn't the clownfish afford a house?
A. Because he didn't have anemone.

**Q. Why are fish boots the warmest
ones to wear?**
A. Because they have electric 'eels.

Q. Why are goldfish orange?
A. Because the water makes them rusty.

**Q. What's the difference between a fish
and a piano?**
A. You can't tuna fish.

Q. Which day do fish hate the most?
A. Fry-day.

HUMPHREY'S FISHY FUN
Mixed-up fish

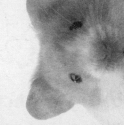

All these MIXED-UP words are parts of a fish's body. Can you unscramble them and write the words in the spaces? Then draw a line to the right part of the body.

YEE
EYE

NIF
FLN

THUMO
MOUTH

LESSAC
SCALES

ILAT
TAIL

Fish word ladder

Hmmm, this word ladder starts and ends with 'FISH', but all the words in between are missing. Read the clues to guess the word but remember — only change ONE letter each time.

1. Something that a fairy might grant you.

2. Something you do if you want to get clean.

3. Something you can do to potatoes if you like them soft and creamy.

4. Part of a ship.

5. The opposite of 'first'.

6. Something that you write to help you remember all your shopping.

7. What your hand is called when it is curled up in a ball.

8. A pet that loves water!

FISH

1. WISH
2. WASH
3. MASH
4. MASI
5. LASI
6. LIST
7. EIST
8. FISH

FISH

Fishy dot-to-dot

Here comes something colourful and lovely to look at. In fact, this pet is just an ANGEL! When you've joined the dots, why not decorate it with lots of colourful stripes and spots?

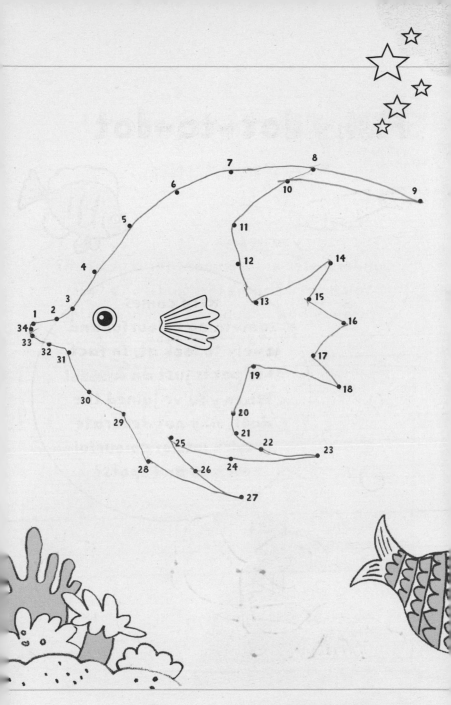

Design an aquarium

Can you design a FANTASTIC underwater environment for a pet fish? You'll need things for the fish to swim through and around, as well as making the tank look good.

UNUSUAL PETS

You wouldn't be at all surprised about seeing a cat, a dog or a hamster in someone's house. But you might be a little taken aback to see stick insects, lizards, frogs, snakes or spiders! These kinds of unusual pets are also known as 'exotic' pets, and while they're not as cute and cuddly as the more common household pets, they do appeal to quite a lot of people.

Looking after an unusual pet might sound like a really fun thing to do, but the decision needs a lot of careful thought. Many of these creatures are wild animals who are not used to living in houses or gardens and they need special environments created for them if they are to be healthy, happy and well.

You will need to do a lot of research beforehand and find out about *everything* the creature needs to have a happy life, and whether you and your family can really provide these things. Remember that there are many unwanted exotic pets being looked after by animal rescue shelters. These are pets that people have bought with every good intention but who have sadly ended up in a rescue home because their owners realised that they could not look after them properly. It's a very good idea to talk to a vet or anyone who has owned the kind of pet you want before making a final decision.

I guess Og the frog is what you call an 'exotic pet'. He certainly is a little UNUSUAL!

Some things to find out if you're thinking of getting an unusual pet:

1. How big will your pet eventually grow?

That tiny snake you buy in a pet shop could grow into a giant! Not only will it be more difficult to handle, it will eat a lot more and will need more living space. You will also need to find out how long the animal is likely to live – some snakes, for example, can live for more than 20 years. Can you imagine looking after a pet for all that time?

2. What does the pet eat?

Would you be willing to handle live insects to feed to your frog or lizard? Or keep a supply of frozen mice to feed your snake? Find out about the animal's diet and where you will get a regular supply of food from.

I'll never forget the first time I saw Og being fed live crickets. EWWW!

3. How much space will it need?

Many people underestimate how much space animals need to live in and, as we all know, it is cruel to keep creatures in spaces that are too small for them. Most pet birds, for example, should not be kept in small cages but need to live in proper aviaries with space to fly around. Does your family have the space to build the right kind of enclosure?

4. What kind of enclosure will it live in?

Most exotic animals need carefully controlled environments, as many come from countries with different climates and landscapes to ours. Creating and maintaining this kind of environment takes a lot of work. For example, a garter snake will

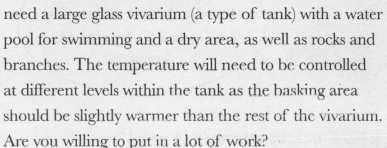

need a large glass vivarium (a type of tank) with a water pool for swimming and a dry area, as well as rocks and branches. The temperature will need to be controlled at different levels within the tank as the basking area should be slightly warmer than the rest of the vivarium. Are you willing to put in a lot of work?

Mr Brisbane is a person who puts in a LOT of effort. He even built Og his very own swimming pool!

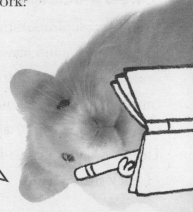

5. How much time will I need?

Probably more than you think!
Once you have set up the proper
environment, your pet will need
feeding, her home will need cleaning
out and there will be other essential
tasks to perform. This takes longer with exotic pets
as there is more to think about. For example, some
creatures need lighting turned on and off at different
times of day and constant temperature regulation.
Stick insects, for example, need to be sprayed with
water several times a day.

6. How much will it cost?

Buying and looking after exotic pets can be incredibly
expensive. They usually need special enclosures and
special foods, and there might also be energy bills for
keeping their enclosures at the right temperature.
If your pet is sick, the vet's bills might cost a lot.
You will also need to have a specialist vet within
reach of your house.

7. Where does it come from?

Some animals, even ones you can buy in pet shops, are illegally transported from their native lands and can be treated cruelly during this process. You need to make sure that you are buying a pet that has been bred in captivity but that has been not taken away from its parents sooner than it should. Also bear in mind that some exotic pets need special licences before you are allowed to keep them – another thing to find out in advance.

If you've considered all the above and still want to go ahead, do your research thoroughly and work out a proper care programme for your unusual pet with your family. Or you could maybe ask your school if it is possible to have a pet such as a frog or

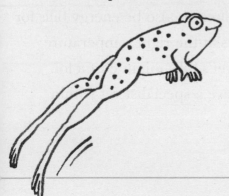

a stick insect in the classroom, and share the care among your classmates.

Og the frog and I are very well looked after by our friends in Room 26. They share the responsibility and make sure no one forgets their jobs. THANKS-THANKS-THANKS!

Don't be too disappointed if it isn't possible for you to have exactly the pet you want – you can always go and see the more unusual creatures at zoos and at least know that they are getting the proper care there. Perhaps you could choose a pet that is easier to look after? How about a hamster?!

Unusual pet facts

* Tarantula spiders shed their furry skins as they grow, leaving behind what looks like another tarantula.
* The largest African giant land snail ever recorded was called Gee Geronimo. It was 15 inches (38cm) long and weighed 2 pounds (0.91kg).
* Stick insects come in all sizes. Some are tiny, just half an inch long (just over 1cm), other types can grow much bigger. One of the largest in the world is the *Phobaeticus kirbyi*, which comes from Borneo. One example was found to be over 21 inches (about 55cm) long, with its legs outstretched!

Now I don't think even Og, with his super-long tongue, could manage THAT for a snack!

✱ It's possible to buy tiny green frogs called 'Pixie frogs' in some pet shops. Despite the cute name, they are actually baby African bullfrogs, one of the largest frogs in South Africa. They can grow to 9.5 inches (24cm) and may even end up weighing over 2 kilograms! They eat bugs, fish, mice, lizards – and occasionally other frogs. If the African bullfrog becomes scared or feels threatened it puffs itself right up.

When OG the frog first arrived at Longfellow School, he was put in a tank with a bullfrog called George. Well, George didn't like it one bit! That's how Og got put in Room 26 with me. I think he prefers me to George. Who wouldn't?

✳ Some types of snake, such as vipers, boas and pythons, have special temperature-sensing organs located between their eyes and nostrils. These organs are sensitive to very tiny changes in temperature and help the snake to navigate and hunt down warm-blooded prey in the dark.

✳ Certain types of snake can escape enemies by 'playing dead'. If it is threatened by a predator the snake flips on to its back, opens its mouth and allows its tongue to loll in a convincingly dead manner. To make sure the predator keeps right away, it might also release a horrible-smelling substance from its glands.

✳ Some lizards have also evolved a unique way to get away from predators. When attacked, they are able to separate their tail from the rest of their body! The predator often feasts on the still-wriggling tail while the lizard makes its escape. Later, the lizard simply grows a new tail – which is usually shorter and differently coloured.

✱ Turtles are thought to have been on the earth for more than 200 million years. They evolved before mammals, birds, crocodiles, snakes and lizards and were around when dinosaurs existed. Some species of turtles can live to be over a hundred years of age.

✱ The Madagascar hissing cockroach is known for the distinctive noise it makes. The loud hissing can be heard when the males fight with each other. This type of cockroach has 'horns' which it uses in combat to ram its opponent.

I'm really glad my class doesn't keep hissing cockroaches. It took me long enough to get used to Og's 'BOING'!

Humphrey on frogs

As you all know, when a certain noisy frog first arrived in Room 26 I wasn't sure if I liked him — but I'm so glad we got to know each other because he's now one of my best pals! And since then I've found out a whole lot more about FROGS and how they live. Here are some of the things I've discovered.

✱ Some frogs can jump distances up to 20 times their own body length in a single leap!

✱ Og is a type of frog called *Rana clamitans* – otherwise known as a green frog. Green frogs are found in the eastern half of the United States and can be green or brownish in colour. They are about 5–10 cm (2–4 inches) in length and live in shallow fresh water. Green frogs will eat anything that they can swallow: insects, worms and sometimes fish. Their distinctive call has been compared to the plunking sound of a loose banjo string!

I knew I'd heard that 'BOING!' somewhere before!

* Frogs like a varied diet and most will eat crickets, locusts, earthworms, cockroaches and mealworms. The larger varieties of frog will even eat pinky mice. Never over-feed a pet frog, as he can get obese.

* Frogs are amphibians, and most of them live part of their life in water and part on land. Amphibians are cold-blooded animals. This means that their body temperature adjusts to the temperature of their surroundings, so they are hot when their environment is hot and cold when their environment is cold.

* Some types of frog live in trees. Tree frogs have special sticky pads on their toes and fingers which help them grip and climb trunks and branches. One of the more popular frogs commonly kept as a pet is called the White's tree frog. Despite their name, these frogs come in different colours, mainly turquoises, greens and browns.

* In many frog species only the males croak – they do this to attract females and to mark their territory. Many kinds of frog can puff themselves up with air when they croak, which makes the noise even louder!

✻ Most frogs don't like being held so only handle your frog if you have to. The salts that are on your skin may irritate him, so always wash your hands before handling a frog, or wear gloves. You'll need to wash your hands afterwards too, as some frogs release a fluid when they are stressed which can be toxic to humans.

That's what happened to Mandy Payne when she picked up Og without permission. Mrs Brisbane sent her to wash her hands. Now she ALWAYS puts on rubber gloves to handle Og.

Ribbit

* As frogs' skin absorbs liquid, they do not need to drink water to survive.

* In English frogs usually say 'Croak' or 'Ribbit'! Take a look at frog sounds in other languages:

Mandarin Chinese: GUO GUO
French: COA-COA
German: QUAA, QUAAK
Hungarian: BRE-KE-KE
Italian: CRA CRA
Japanese: KERO KERO
Korean: GAE-GOOL-GAE-GOOL
Thai: OB OB
Turkish: VRAK VRAK

JOKING AROUND WITH HUMPHREY

Q. Why is the letter 't' so important to a stick insect?
A. Because without 't', it would be a sick insect.

Q. What do you get if you cross a tarantula with a rose?
A. I don't know, but i wouldn't try smelling it!

Q. What do you call a lizard that sings?
A. A rap-tile.

Q. What do snakes write on cards?
A. 'With love and hisses'.

Q. Which snakes are the best at sums?
A. Adders.

Q. When is a car like a frog?
A. When it's being toad.

That joke is
'TOAD-ally' terrible!

Q. Why did the tadpole feel lonely?
A. He was newt to the area.

Q. How do snails get their shells so shiny?
A. They use snail varnish.

HUMPHREY'S UNUSUAL PET FUN

Weird pet wordsearch

A whole lot of UNUSUAL pets are hiding in this wordsearch. Can you find them?

SNAKE • LIZARD • NEWT
SPIDER • STICK INSECT • SNAIL
FROG • TOAD

S	B	H	L	G	S	E	F	O	A	T
N	E	W	T	S	A	O	K	N	C	M
A	L	M	O	D	S	F	O	E	I	F
I	O	K	U	L	P	A	S	A	U	W
L	U	D	A	B	S	N	A	K	E	K
N	F	R	O	G	I	K	D	Q	O	R
O	P	A	U	K	U	I	A	N	W	E
C	N	Z	C	I	C	S	L	B	I	D
W	E	I	K	T	H	T	O	A	D	I
Q	T	L	S	U	S	J	P	S	N	P
S	O	G	I	J	F	R	O	D	H	S

Snake wordsnake

I've heard you can never fool a snake — it's IMPOSSIBLE to pull their legs!

Can you find all these snakes in the grid opposite? Use a pencil to draw a continuous line through the words, which 'snake' around, up and down, backwards and forwards, but never diagonally. The words are in the same order as the list below.

COBRA • VIPER • PYTHON
BOA CONSTRICTOR • ANACONDA
ADDER • RATTLESNAKE
MAMBA • GARTERSNAKE

C	O	B	E	K	A	N
V	A	R	T	E	R	S
I	R	P	R	A	G	A
P	E	Y	M	A	M	B
A	O	T	E	K	A	N
C	B	H	D	E	E	S
O	N	O	D	R	L	T
N	S	T	A	R	A	T
C	I	R	A	D	N	O
T	O	R	A	N	A	C

Humphrey's Unusual Pet Fun   189

Frog dot-to-dot

Here's a VERY good friend of mine! Can you fill in his bubble with his usual sound?

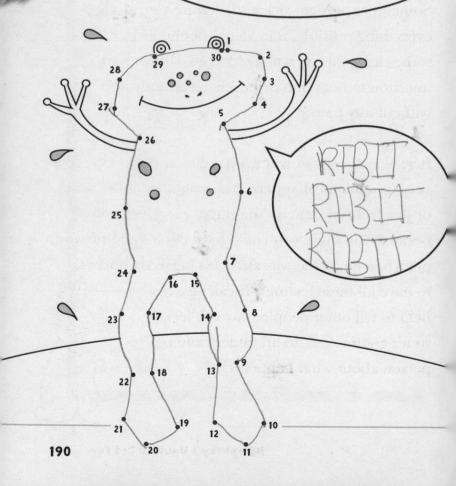

RIBIT
RIBIT
RIBIT

A good life

Lots of kids spend many happy years with their pets. But pets can't always be with us forever. Some animals do lead long lives but, sadly, many others don't, so they may die sooner than you expect. Sometimes pets get sick and, despite your doing everything possible, they might not get better. In some cases, the vet will need to give the pet an injection to help him or her die peacefully and without any pain.

It's always very sad when a pet dies and you may feel very upset if this happens. You might feel like crying or just feel very lonely. You might even feel guilty because you think you could have done more for your pet when he or she was alive. It's perfectly normal to have all these feelings. It can also really help to tell other people how you feel, so it's good to talk to an understanding person about what happened.

It's comforting to remember all the happy times you had with your pet. You could also think of ways of saying goodbye to your friend, e.g.

✱ Remember funny stories about your pet and make a scrapbook of pictures, photos and memories about their life.

✱ Have a burial ceremony for your pet to say goodbye and to celebrate their life.

✱ Write a poem or story about your pet or about how you feel.

> I know how it feels to be unsqueakably SAD-SAD-SAD. And how it feels to miss someone. Sometimes I write little poems in my notebook and it really helps me.

HUMPHREY'S AMAZING PETS

> You know, I've heard some GREAT stories about pets from all around the world. Aldo read some out to me from the newspaper and some of the students in Room 26 have told me a few.
> Here are some of my favourites!

Brave Beasts

The PDSA Dickin Medal is a special award given to animals that show incredible bravery. It was founded during the Second World War (1939–45) in honour of the animals who helped humans.

During the war, five dogs in London received the medal by helping to find and rescue people buried under rubble during heavy bombing. Hundreds of lives were saved, thanks to these courageous canines.

Doggy descents

Another dog, Rob, got the medal for keeping guard over soldiers who were behind enemy lines on important wartime missions. How did this plucky dog reach the soldiers? Rob was parachuted down! He made 20 parachute descents in total during the Second World War.

The courageous cat

Many medal winners have been dogs, but pigeons, horses and even one cat have also been recipients! During the war, Simon was the ship's cat on board HMS *Amethyst* which came under attack on the Yangtze River in China. The captain was killed and the ship was then trapped on the river under fire by the Chinese for 100 days. There wasn't much food left, but Simon protected the men's rations by catching the rats that

overran the ship. He was also a great comfort
to the frightened soldiers on board the ship. Simon
was awarded the Dickin Medal in November 1949.

The faithful guides

Much more recently, two Labrador guide dogs, Salty and
Roselle, were awarded the medal after they led their blind
owners to safety out of the World Trade Center following
the terrorist attack on New York on 11 September 2001.
The dogs carefully took their owners all the way down
the chaotic, smoke-filled stairs, passing a total of 70
floors. They were praised for their courage and devotion.

My own personal
bravery award goes to
Og — for jumping all the way
out of his tank and rescuing me
when I was trapped under a
bag of Nutri-Nibbles. He even
let me ride on his back like a
bucking bronco! That
frog is something
SPECIAL!

A bunny hero

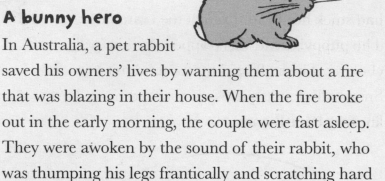

In Australia, a pet rabbit
saved his owners' lives by warning them about a fire
that was blazing in their house. When the fire broke
out in the early morning, the couple were fast asleep.
They were awoken by the sound of their rabbit, who
was thumping his legs frantically and scratching hard
on their bedroom door. It was only then that they
realised smoke was billowing through the house. They
escaped but the firefighters said that they were very
lucky to have been warned by their helpful pet.

Guinea pig alert

A guinea pig called Snowball saved the life of a
puppy called Bianca while they were both being
kept in an animal shelter. The staff at the shelter
were alerted by a frantic squealing from Snowball's
hutch and rushed to check on her. However, it
wasn't Snowball who was having a problem. They
immediately saw that a puppy dog in a crate just
across the hall from Snowball had tried to escape and

had stuck her head through the crate door. The puppy's head was trapped and she was choking. The staff said that if it hadn't been for Snowball's loud squeals, they would never have known about Bianca.

Wow! I've done some daring things in my time. I once swung from a high cord to get back into my cage — that was scary! And I pinged Clem the dog on the nose with a rubber band. That got rid of him! But these animals are really BRAVE-BRAVE-BRAVE!

Psychic Pets

Do some animals 'know' things that humans don't? The idea that animals can predict earthquakes has been around for centuries. Reports of dogs, cats, horses, chickens and many other animals behaving strangely, becoming restless or suddenly leaving the area just before an earthquake occurs are common around the world. Even as long ago as 373 BC, it was recorded that hundreds of rats, snakes, centipedes and weasels deserted the Greek city of Helice, just days before an earthquake happened! More recently, a scientist who was researching toads in Italy thought it strange that a whole colony of toads had suddenly abandoned their home. Three days later, an earthquake struck. The toads only returned ten days after the quake.

So how do the animals know something that we can't predict? It's a mystery that has puzzled scientists for a long time. One theory is that animals have superior senses to humans and can perhaps feel the earth's vibrations before a quake. The other theory says that animals might be able to detect electrical changes in the air that happen before an earthquake. Or do animals have a kind of 'sixth sense' that we don't know about?

I can feel all kinds of vibrations in the air with my whiskers but I don't know if I could detect an EARTHQUAKE. I hope I never get the chance to find out!

The lucky cat

If you ever visit Japan, you will notice that there are colourful little cat ornaments everywhere in windows and entrances of shops and restaurants. The reason for displaying these 'lucky cats' is because of a real cat who saved a human's life because she knew that something bad was about to happen. The story goes that a man once saw a cat waving a paw at him and was so amazed that he went over to have a closer look. As he moved away, a bolt of lightning struck the place where he had been standing! As the cat saved his life, she has been known as the 'lucky' cat ever since. The cat – called the maneki-neko – is usually sitting up with one paw raised as if saying 'hello' or beckoning to you.

Faithful pets

There are several stories of loving and loyal dogs who have never forgotten their owners.

Greyfriars Bobby

Bobby was a Skye terrier whose owner, John Gray, died in February 1858 in Edinburgh, Scotland. Bobby was so devoted to his owner that he sat at his grave every day for 14 years, only leaving to get his lunch at one o'clock every day. The faithful little terrier became very well-known in the area and was given the name 'Greyfriars Bobby', after the cemetery in which his master was buried. Bobby is now buried inside the gate of the same cemetery. There is also a famous statue of him in Edinburgh, which many visitors come to see.

I for one will certainly never forget my first proper owner, the wonderful Ms Mac. When she came back from her travels to see me I was so HAPPY-HAPPY-HAPPY!

Hachiko

There is a similar famous story of a loyal dog, Hachiko, in Japan. Every day Hachiko would accompany his master, a professor, to Shibuya train station where he caught the train for work. At the end of the day Hachiko would always return to the station to greet him. But in May 1925 the professor was taken ill at work and he did not return to the station. He died soon afterwards. Hachiko was given to some relatives to look after but he escaped and made his way to Shibuya station to patiently wait for the professor. He did this every day and became a well-known visitor. People began bringing Hachiko snacks to eat. After ten years of waiting, Hachiko eventually died, in the same spot, still waiting for his friend to return. Today a statue stands in the place where Hachiko waited.

Wacky pets

The White House 'Zoo'

Many US Presidents have kept dogs and cats at the White House, but former President Calvin Coolidge was surely the biggest pet fanatic ever. As well as dogs, cats and birds, he kept two raccoons, a donkey called Ebenezer, a bobcat named Smoky and a pygmy hippopotamus called Billy. The President was also given several exotic animals as gifts during his time in office, including two lion cubs, a wallaby and a black bear! President Obama's daughters, Malia and Sasha, have just one pet, a very cute black Portuguese water dog called Bo.

I'd REALLY like to have a good run around the White House. I hear it's very spacious but I'm not sure if I'd want to bump into Bo, cute or not!

Chew on this!

A chewy hamster called Samantha created mayhem before she even reached her new home. Samantha was bought from a pet shop in England, but she disappeared in the car on the way to her new owner's house. The family searched everywhere but just couldn't find any trace of the little rodent. When the car wouldn't start the next day, it was taken to a garage where they found Samantha hidden behind the dashboard. She had eaten right through the ignition cable! The mechanics put the hamster in a cardboard box but she ate through that as well. So she ended up in a toolbox with an apple to chew on until her owner arrived to finally take her to her new home.

I was driven in a car from Pet-O-Rama, the pet shop where Ms Mac first bought me. But I didn't even THINK about escaping — I was so excited to see what my new home was going to be like!

MY STAR PET

Everyone's pet is special to them but what's so special about your pet? Does he/she have any funny habits or clever tricks? Have there been any interesting incidents or stories that have happened to your pet?

Write down all the things that make your pet unique.

She gives me kisses
Rubs my face with her
paw when I hold her
like a baby and I
rub her face

You and your pet

Whichever kind of pet you choose to own, the most important thing to remember is that he or she will depend on you completely, for everything they need to survive. Before you own a pet, you must be really, really sure that you will ALWAYS remember to feed them, clean them out and make sure that they are exercised and entertained. Every single day! Even when you don't feel like it or you would rather go and do something else.

No one takes better care of pets than Golden Miranda. She would never forget to feed or clean out her pets. And she has lovely golden hair — like ME!

My pet's routine

What does my pet eat?

Cat meat and cat biscets

How many times a day does my pet feed?

3 for now

How often does its home need cleaning out?

cage needs cleaning out
(a day (all of it)

When does my pet sleep?

12:00 noon for 3-4 hours

What kind of exercise does my pet take?

running around going crazy

What does my pet do for fun?

chews your finger or grooms
you

You and your family will also need to think carefully about who will look after your pet if you go away on holiday. Hopefully, you will know someone who loves animals as much as you do and will be happy to take good care of them.

It's up to you to find out as much as you possibly can about your pet and his individual needs. This book is a great start, but there are many other ways of finding out more about different creatures:
✼ Many animal welfare organisations have excellent advice on their websites.
✼ There are lots of good books about individual pets and how to look after them in libraries and bookshops.
✼ You can ask people such as vets or knowledgeable pet shop staff for advice.

Your pet is also an individual with his own likes and dislikes. As you spend more time together you will gradually get to know your pet's personality and quirky little ways – it's all part of the fun of owning a pet!

It's been UNSQUEAKABLY fun for me to learn all about humans. Pets are like humans, too — they come in lots of different shapes, sizes and colours. And, like humans, they are all really interesting when you get to know them better. So have fun finding out!

ANSWERS

P.77 Furry fun wordsearch

O	E	I	M	J	G	F	R	G	C
L	M	O	U	S	E	B	I	A	H
A	N	P	T	S	E	P	R	H	I
S	T	I	B	B	A	R	E	J	N
B	C	H	F	E	R	K	T	L	C
O	B	D	N	W	M	I	S	C	H
M	E	I	L	L	V	T	M	N	I
B	U	S	A	Q	U	A	A	H	L
G	E	R	B	I	L	G	H	D	L
I	C	P	G	X	E	A	I	N	A

P.80 Rodent shadow match 1b, 2e, 3a, 4d, 5c

P.77 Rabbit word challenge

SIT, BIT, BITS, SAT, BAT, BATS, STIR, STAB, BAR, BARS, ART, ARTS, BRAT, BRATS, RIB, RIBS, BAIT, BAITS, STAIR, TAR, TAB, TABS

P.77 Bunny brainpower crossword

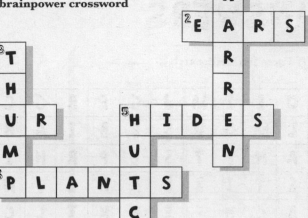

Across:
2. EARS
4. FUR
5. HIDES
6. PLANTS

Down:
1. WARREN
3. THUMB
5. HUTCH

P.120 Cat know-how

1. Sleeping, 2. Scratching,
3. Grooming, 4. Claws,
5. Whiskers, 6. Tail,
7. Meow, 8. Purr, 9. Hiss

P.122 Cat word grid

1. LICK
2. FISH
3. TAIL
4. HUNT
5. FLEA
6. NAP

P.142 Doggy wordsnake

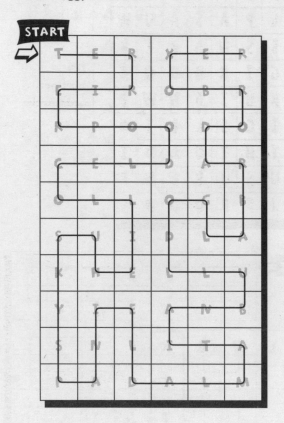

P.161 Mixed-up fish

EYE, FIN, MOUTH, SCALES, TAIL

P.162 Fish word ladder

Answers: WISH, WASH, MASH, MAST, LAST, LIST, FIST, FISH.

P. 186
Weird pet wordsearch

P. 188 Snake wordsnake

START ⟹

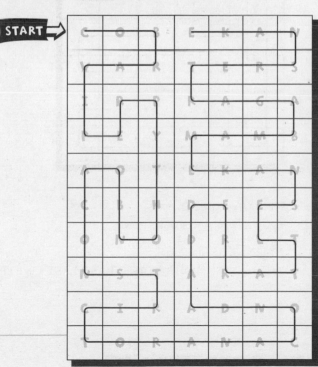

Look for my book of
unsqueakably funny jokes

Or why not try the
puzzles and games in my
fun-fun-fun activity
book!

Puzzles and Games

From everybody's favourite hamster:

ME!!

Secret Codes!

Jokes!

Puzzles!

Humphrey's
Book of
Fun-Fun-Fun

ff   Betty G. Birney

The World According to Humphrey

Betty G. Birney

ff

Dear Friends,

When I first arrived at Longfellow School, I was unsqueakably happy! After all, the life of a classroom pet is FUN-FUN-FUN!

However, going home each weekend with a different student turned out to be quite a challenge, because humans need a lot of help! Along the way, I learned to shoot rubber bands at a nosy dog, teach a shy girl to squeak up for herself, help the caretaker find true love and star in the Halloween party. I really had my paws full . . . especially since the teacher, Mrs. Brisbane, was definitely out to get me! (It makes my whiskers quiver just to think about it!)

Your friend always,

Humphrey

Out Now!

Friendship According to Humphrey

Betty G. Birney   ff

Dear Friends,

I was green with envy when Og the Frog moved into Room 26. He had no fur at all and wasn't a bit friendly. My fellow students were all having problems with their friends, too. It took a clever hamster (me) to set things straight and a lumpy green frog to teach me the true meaning of friendship.

Your friend to the end,

Humphrey

Out Now!

Betty G. Birney

Dear Friends,

Trouble was brewing all over Room 26. I was GLAD-GLAD-GLAD that my friends named their model town after me. But I was SAD-SAD-SAD that Golden-Miranda was in big trouble and it was all my fault! I just had to help her, even if it meant I'd be locked up forever.

Your funny, furry friend,

Humphrey

Out Now!

Humphrey and his friends have been hard at work making a brand new FUN-FUN-FUN website just for you!

Play Humphrey's exciting new game, share your pet pictures, find fun crafts and activities, read Humphrey's very own diary and discover all the latest news from your favourite furry friend at:

www.funwithhumphrey.com

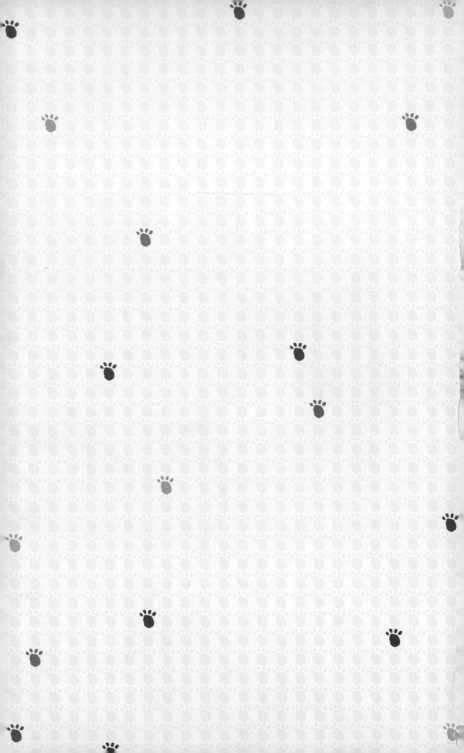